P U B W A

— I N —

Cambridgeshire

THIRTY CIRCULAR WALKS
AROUND CAMBRIDGESHIRE INNS

Jean and Geoff Pratt

COUNTRYSIDE BOOKS
NEWBURY, BERKSHIRE

COUNTRYSIDE BOOKS
3 Catherine Road
Newbury, Berkshire

ISBN 1 85306 327 4

Designed by Mon Mohan
Cover illustration by Colin Doggett
Photographs and maps by the authors

Produced through MRM Associates Ltd., Reading
Typeset by The Midlands Book Typesetting Company, Loughborough
Printed by J W Arrowsmith Ltd, Bristol

Contents

Publisher's Note

We hope that you obtain considerable enjoyment from this book; great care has been taken in its preparation. However, changes of landlord and actual closure are sadly not uncommon. Likewise, although at the time of publication all routes followed public rights of way or permitted paths, diversion orders can be made and permissions withdrawn.

We cannot of course be held responsible for such diversion orders and any resultant inaccuracies in the text which result from these or any other changes to the routes nor any damage which might result from walkers trespassing on private property. We are anxious that all details covering the walks and the pubs are kept up to date and would therefore welcome information from readers which would be relevant to future editions.

Introduction

Modern Cambridgeshire comprises what was formerly four separate counties: Cambridgeshire, Huntingdonshire, the Isle of Ely and the Soke of Peterborough.

The city of Cambridge lies on the river Cam, near the southern edge of the great area of fenland which stretches to the north and east into Lincolnshire and Norfolk ending at the Wash. The drainage of the Fens, which has occurred through several centuries of agricultural development, has resulted in the present characteristic landscape of this part of Cambridgeshire, where parallel drainage ditches criss-cross the land. The history and various aspects of the drainage of the Fens are introduced and described in the separate walks. The land in the southern part of the county has a very different character. Here there are rolling chalky downs, rounded hills and shallow valleys. Western Cambridgeshire is a stretch of slightly higher land along which the Great North Road, now called the A1 but in Roman times known as Ermine Street, formed a major trading route from London to Yorkshire and Scotland. Towards the north-west corner of the county, small villages with stone-built dwellings nestle in shallow valleys. Here there is limestone and in times past there was a major industry in quarrying. No more is stone won from the area, but to the east of Peterborough are large brickworks supplying the whole country.

With drainage the marshy fens have now given way to rich, fertile, peaty land. Peat is like a sponge and as it dries out it shrinks. In many places in Cambridgeshire you will be aware that the level of the land is way below the level of the rivers and drainage ditches, their water being held in by high banks. The shrinkage of the peat is shown dramatically at the site of the Holme Fen Posts, in Holme Fen, which lies to the east of the A1 in the north-west of the county. They are worth a visit. As none of the walks in this book actually passes the spot, we have mentioned the Holme Fen Posts in both the Stilton and Ramsey walks, as being the two closest points visited.

The 30 walks in this book have been chosen for a variety of reasons. In each case it has been our aim to find an interesting circular walk of about 4 to 5 miles in length, through pleasant country, starting and finishing at a comfortable country pub where tasty and varied food and drink are offered.

Except where the use of a permissive path is mentioned in the walk description, all the routes followed are on public rights of way shown officially on the definitive map. A permissive path is one where an owner has given permission for a path to be used by the public.

Area map showing locations of the walks.

Unsurfaced country footpaths and bridleways can be affected by the weather and may be muddy and puddly at times. It is generally advisable to wear stout shoes or boots and be prepared for wet conditions. The rivers of Cambridgeshire being part of the complex land drainage system for much of central England, the watermeadows beside the rivers Great Ouse and Nene, together with the 'washlands' between the Old and New Bedford rivers, are allowed to flood during times of widespread rain. Therefore, in winter, have regard to the possibility of parts of the walks by the rivers being temporarily flooded.

The sketch maps, which are not to scale, do not show all the buildings, hedges, bridges and other details. The information on the maps is intended to help the user interpret the route and confirm the instructions given in the text.

Farmers are forbidden by law to put a bull in a field crossed by a public right of way, unless it is of a recognised beef breed and is accompanied by cows and/or heifers. Such bulls, in these conditions, are thought not to be aggressive. A bull over ten months old must never be on its own in a field crossed by a public right of way. Bull notices are sometimes displayed on gates, but farmers occasionally forget to remove the notice when the bull is taken elsewhere.

Most of the pubs used in the book have ample car parking, and other parking places are mentioned. It is always advisable to seek the agreement of the landlord before leaving a car at the pub whilst away walking. If you park elsewhere than in a public car park, please take care not to cause obstruction to other traffic or to local residents.

Opening times on weekdays vary from pub to pub, however the majority of pubs are open between 11.30 am and 2.30 pm and then between 6.30 pm and 11 pm. Where times differ from these by more than 30 minutes, a comment is made in the pub description. On Sundays, the statutory opening times of 12 noon to 3 pm and 7 pm to 10.30 pm apply. Food is usually served between 12 noon and 2.30 pm and between 6.30 pm and 9.30 pm. Here again, any significant variation from these times is referred to in the text.

We are grateful to Mary Bird who read through the script, commenting in detail on the content and thus improving the flow of the book. Our thanks, too, to members of the Rights of Way staff of the Cambridgeshire County Council whom we have consulted about details of the rights of way, and to Mr Bill Wakefield of Stretham, and Dr Lomas and Dr Hawkins of Little Wilbraham. We are also indebted to the museum staff at St Ives and Wisbech, who have given useful information.

Jean and Geoff Pratt
Spring 1995

Barnack
The Millstone

The Millstone, which has been the village pub since 1672, is a charming warren of small, intimate dining and drinking areas, and, in addition to these, there is a secluded walled garden, set with tables and chairs. A real old-fashioned pub. Gleaming brass and copper utensils, trumpets, carriage horse tack and a yoke for carrying pails decorate the walls. Padded benches and upholstered seats give an air of comfort.

The meals are served in generous portions. Dishes such as gammon and eggs, pies – steak and kidney, steak and mushroom, turkey and mushroom – minted lamb bake, spare ribs in a barbecue sauce, chicken breasts filled with a prawn and lobster sauce, ocean pie and vegetarian dishes, such as leek and mushroom bake, are featured on the menu. Home-made sweets are many and varied. Coffee comes with a wrapped minty chocolate. Real ales, such as Everards Tiger Best Bitter, Everards Old Original, Adnams, Ridleys IPA and a variety of guest beers, are available. Strongbow draught cider is on sale, too. Meals are served at lunchtimes and in the evenings every day, except Sunday evenings and Monday evenings. Dogs are welcome outside the pub, but are not allowed inside. Children can eat in the family room.

Telephone: 01780 740296.

How to get there: Barnack is 3 miles south-east of Stamford. If travelling on the A1 northwards towards Stamford, there is no right turn off the dual-carriageway, so continue to the roundabout at the B1081 for Stamford and go south on the A1. Take the next turning on the left for Barnack. In 1½ miles turn right and then left. In ½ mile go straight on at the crossroads. The Millstone is in Millstone Lane, the next turning on the right.

Parking: Parking can be found beside and behind the pub.

Length of the walk: 3½ miles. Map: OS Landranger sheet 142 Peterborough (inn GR 077049).

At first, this walk wanders through the stone-built village. In School Lane you will pass a 13th century arch, now set in a high stone garden wall, which once was in the wall between the tower and the nave in the parish church. Leaving Barnack along Church Lane, the route continues south to Southorpe, from whence it returns along part of the Hereward Way, a 110 mile footpath from Oakham, going through Peterborough and across the Fens to join the Peddars Way in Norfolk.

The walk ends by going round two sides of the 54 acre nature reserve called, very descriptively, 'Hills and Holes'.

The Walk
Leave the Millstone and go left along Millstone Lane to the T-junction with School Road. Turn right and at the next T-junction go right again, into Jack Haws Lane. Follow the bend round to the left into the Square. Go left beside the Fox and continue, with an attractive high stone wall and garden on your right, towards the church of St John the Baptist.

Beside the post office leave the road, going to the right up a surfaced path between fences, stone walls and later hedges. Follow this path for quite some way. Pass on the right the village cricket ground. By a tall footpath sign snake right a little, with a hedge on the left and a stone wall on the right and beyond that the cricket pavilion. Keep straight on to a wooden kissing-gate alongside the bowling green on your right. In 80 more yards reach a pasture. Continue parallel to the hedge on your left, and when that hedge turns left you carry straight on towards the stone house beside the road at the far side of the field. Away to your right is Walcot Hall.

Leave the pasture by the white wooden kissing-gate, where you will meet a road on a bend. Go left along the road past the stone house, where you go right off the road beside the house, on a footpath across the field, towards some stone houses that you can see in a gap at the far side of the field.

Go over the wooden stile beside the wooden farm gate into a

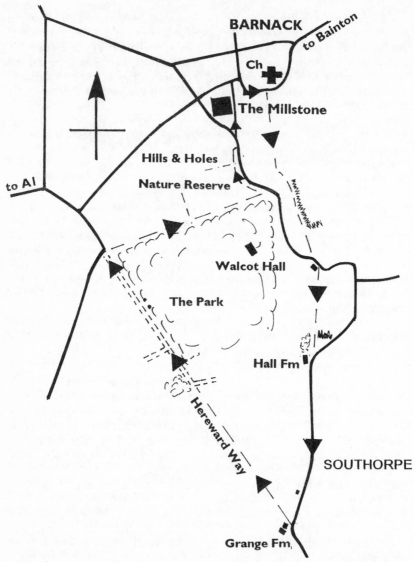

triangular pasture. Head towards the left of the stone barns, where there is a stile in the corner and a white farm gate nearby.

Keep on the footway through the village of Southorpe, with its stone-built houses. Pass Stud Farm on your right and, immediately before Grange Farm, go right, away from the road through a wooden bridlegate by a 'Bridleway' sign.

10

After the second bridlegate you are in a bigger field. Continue in much the same direction as before, not alongside the row of trees but going to the left of two lone oaks, one very stag-headed, in the middle of the field, climbing up a slight bank. Keep in the same general direction, on the slightly higher ground. Ahead, on the far side of the field, you can see a hedge with a big tree and, to the right of it, a small clump of trees. Head for those trees. As you approach, you will find the clump is by the far pointy corner of the field. Go through the bridlegate under the ash tree. Keep straight on, with a low stone wall on your right. This is the Hereward Way.

As the stone wall on your right ends, one on the left comes round a corner to join you. Walk beside it as you meet a chalky farm track at a bend. In 200 yards that wall goes left and a track soon goes left too, but you carry straight on along a grassy-middled track.

Presently you pass two enormous widely-spaced square stone gate pillars, topped with capitals and balls. Through the gap you have a vista of pedimented Walcot Hall at the end of a broad grass sward, backed by an avenue of lime trees. Keeping the dry-stone park wall on your right, continue to the end, leaving by a bridlegate to meet a road at a bend. In 20 yards turn right at the corner of the wall, going over a low barrier and again following the wall on your right.

As you pass under the grid lines and the wall changes direction slightly, you can see away on your left the black weather-boarded windmill with its pleasing ogee'd white cap.

By a pedestrian gate enter the nature reserve, and still follow the stone wall on your right. Go through a gate into another part of the reserve. When you reach the wooden kissing-gate by the road opposite the bowling green do not go out to the road, but turn left to follow the permissive path through the Hills and Holes.

As the perimeter path twists and turns and goes up and down over the hills and the holes, you will not be far from the road. Ignore, on the right, first a gate leading to a small layby on the road and then a farm gate and a pedestrian gate, both of which go out to the road. In a few yards go through a small gate into another section of the reserve and continue on a grassy path through the nature reserve, to leave by a further kissing-gate which takes you out to a layby beside the road.

Cross the road to a footway and turn left. Where the road divides, by a thatched house, go straight ahead and very soon arrive back at the Millstone.

2 Kimbolton
The Saddle

Kimbolton, on the western side of Cambridgeshire, lies close to the Bedfordshire border. It is a compact village. The wide main street is flanked with a variety of attractive old buildings tightly packed together, which gives it the air of a town square. At the eastern end it makes a sharp left, and then right, turn to skirt the edge of Kimbolton Castle which dominates the village. This is a large mansion attributed to the 18th century architect, Vanbrugh. Once a stately home, the building has, for many years, housed Kimbolton School. Several modern school buildings have been erected in the grounds.

Midway along the High Street stands the Saddle. The narrow frontage belies the space inside, for the pub goes a long way back. As befits an inn called the Saddle, a good deal of the decoration on the walls is to do with horses. There are riding hats, horse brasses, stirrups and other bits of tack, but pride of place goes to a saddle on an iron frame. Besides that there are plenty of prints of railway engines and framed old maps. On cold days a log fire burns.

It is a cheery place, with prompt service. To eat, there is delicious home-made soup or stuffed mushrooms filled with cream cheese, which can be followed with beef or chicken curry, or steaks grilled with diane or peppercorn sauce, or pan-fried liver with onion rings, chips and peas or a variety of vegetarian dishes. Treacle pudding or other sweets can round off the meal. Children have their own menu to suit their tastes, and are welcome to use the garden. Food is available at lunchtime every day, and every evening except on Sundays. Real ales are served, for instance Tetley, Tolly Cobbold and Bass. Dry Blackthorn cider is on draught. Dogs are welcome when no meals are being served.

Telephone: 01480 860408.

How to get there: Kimbolton is 7 miles north-west of St Neots. From the A1, which bypasses St Neots, take the B645 road leading towards Rushden and Higham Ferrers and pass through the village of Great Staughton. Kimbolton is a further 2 miles and the Saddle is in the main street.

Parking: The main street is very wide and provides plenty of parking.

Length of the walk: 4 miles. Map OS Landranger sheet 153 Bedford, Huntingdon and surrounding area (inn GR 100677).

Passing close to the entrance to the castle, the walk crosses Kimbolton Park to Park Farm and then takes headland paths to a road, Park Lane, at the edge of the Bedfordshire village of Pertenhall. The return is along a broad cart track to College Farm, then to the river Kym, the hamlet of Stonely, and back to the start.

The Walk
From the Saddle go left along the main street and at the end turn right into Castle Green. Go between the huge entrance pillars in the high brick walls, and walk ahead to the left of the large roundabout, with a classroom block on your left and the long, low Donaldson Laboratories to your right. Go straight on to a farm gate, and over the stile to the right of it. Climb up the hill on the marked path towards the right of the brick building seen on the skyline.

Near the top go over the stile affixed to the farm gate and then veer a little to the right, following the fence and passing Park Farm on your left. Several young horse chestnut trees have been planted here. Looking back, enjoy the fine views over Kimbolton.

Join a skew track and follow it leftish. Go over the stile by the double farm gate and go straight ahead on a wide track, passing a cottage on your left, with woods to your right. At the end of the first field go left, with a hedge on your left and open field on your right. Ahead, about 3 miles off, you can pick out the spire of Keysoe church.

When the shelter belt ends take the path that goes left over a two-step stile. At first there is a hedge and a fence to your right, later a fence only.

13

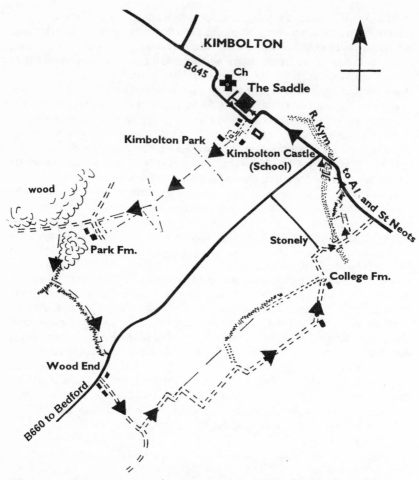

There are fine views from up here. Eventually you go over a stile onto a road, and you will observe that you have already come 1¼ miles.

Turn right along the road for about 200 yards and then left onto a surfaced track beside Lye House. Pass a black weather-boarded barn and a cottage, and carry on along the firm, grassy-middled track, with an erratic hedge on the right, which forms the county boundary with Bedfordshire.

Just before the track bends quite sharply right, turn left at the T-junction and walk down that track. In about 250 yards the track bends right and left. About 50 yards thereafter, the track makes another bend to the right. From this point the official right of way goes straight on across a culvert and across a large field towards College Farm.

The route of the right of way does not seem to be used. The farmer has given permission to continue along the hard farm track and local people take this track. Therefore, if the way across the field is not clear, continue on the farm track round several bends, to pass in about ¾ mile a large grey barn. Snake to the left of it and carry on towards the gap in the high hedge. Pass College Farm on your right.

Curve left, rejoining the definitive right of way, and then right on the farm drive, out to a road at the edge of the village of Stonely. Go right on a path, passing a bench, and cross the footbridge over the river Kym, which leads into a narrow road. Some 100 yards from the bridge and just after a brick pumping station on the right, and by a waymarked electricity pole on the left, go left through the hedge and over a stile.

Follow the fence on the right across the pasture and cross another stile. Keep straight ahead and meet the fence and hedge swinging towards you from the left. Continue beside the hedge and, just before you reach a chestnut tree on the right, go left through the hedge at a waymark. Turn right and follow the hedge on the right out to a road (the B645).

Turn left on the footway and in 100 yards turn left and cross the Kym on a long footbridge. Turn right on a tarmac road which joins the B645.

Walk along the footway parallel to the road. Pass some houses and cross the road that goes to Bedford, then walk beside the high brick wall and the large decorative gates of Kimbolton Castle. Go alongside the ha-ha, round the corner, left, into London Road, and very soon turn right into East Street. That leads you at the end, left, into St Andrews Lane, past the church, with its three levels of lucarnes in the elegant broach spire, back to the High Street and the Saddle.

Castor
The Fitzwilliam Arms

③

The river Nene, from its source near Northampton, passes through Peterborough, before crossing the fens of north Cambridgeshire and out to the sea at the Wash. In the past a route for cargo barges, in these days it is well used by recreational narrow boats and other pleasure craft. Castor and its twin village of Ailsworth, both a few miles west of Peterborough, lie in the broad, shallow valley of the Nene which flows round a series of great loops to the centre of the city. The riverside meadows form an enormous recreational area. The Ferry Meadows Country Park has lakes for wild life and watersports, woods and nature reserves. At one time the river was also a source of water-power. Castor had its watermill, as did Water Newton on the opposite bank.

While the church is the oldest building in Castor, the second oldest is the 400 year old thatched Fitzwilliam Arms. The wide-fronted pub stands back from the road behind a broad forecourt. Although the public can wander through the whole, it is subdivided, each part with its own character. You will find low beams, settles, a window seat and red plush upholstery.

The extensive English and Continental menu includes gammon steak, 16 oz rump steak, chicken Kiev, sweet and sour battered chicken, stuffed plaice with prawns and mushrooms, mackerel salad, double cheeseburger, pan-fried tuna steak, Cumberland sausage and a mixed grill. If you want more, you can choose from caramel apple granny, Mississippi mud pie, Death-by-Chocolate, lemon meringue, blackcurrant cheesecake and apple strudel. Such real ales as Ansells Bitter, Burton Ale and Tetley Bitter are available. You can also buy Olde English draught cider. Meals are served at lunchtimes and in the evenings throughout the week. Children dining with their parents are welcome. They can also play in the large garden at the rear. Dogs, however, are not allowed on the premises.

Telephone: 01733 380251.

How to get there: Castor is 4 miles west of the centre of Peterborough. From a roundabout on the A47, 1½ miles east of the A1 interchange at Wansford, take the minor road to Ailsworth and Castor. You reach the Fitzwilliam Arms in about 1½ miles. Alternatively, from Peterborough follow the A47 and just beyond the town take the slip road to Castor.

Parking: Cars can be parked on the pub forecourt or behind the pub. The street is fairly wide, but somewhat bendy.

Length of the walk: 5½ miles. Map: OS Landranger sheet 142 Peterborough (inn GR 123985).

At first the walk goes across the meadows to Water Newton Mill, a delightful building beside the river, now converted to dwellings. The route then follows the bank of the river Nene along part of the Nene Way, a 111-mile long distance riverside trail from near Daventry to Sutton Bridge, by the Wash. The riverside path is close to the line of the Nene Valley Railway, a private railway line which runs from Wansford to Peterborough. Steam and diesel locomotives can be seen from time to time. The return is along a grassy lane called Landy Green Way.

The Walk

From the Fitzwilliam Arms turn right along the village street for about 150 yards. Turn left opposite a street called The Green, along a tarmac road. Where the tarmac ends bear left and then right along a cinder track which is signed 'Footpath to Water Newton'. Pass the local cricket club on the right. At the end of the track turn right beside a wide ditch known as Splash Dyke.

In 50 yards turn left over a bridge crossing the dyke and swing half-right on a broad grass path between crops. At the far side of the second field bear right beside the Nene Valley Railway. The path leads to the end of a tarmac road. Turn left and cross the railway. On the far side of the line go straight on through a green pedestrian gate into a

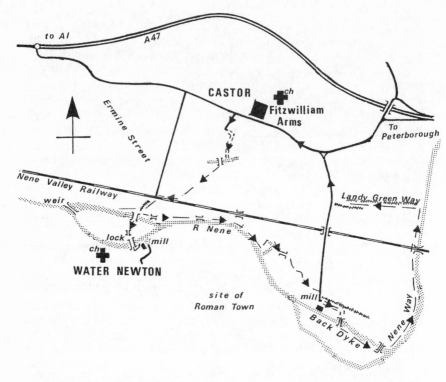

triangular shaped field and keep beside the hedge on the right. Ahead you can see, ¼ mile away, the three-storey Water Newton Mill. Cross a stile to a large steel cartbridge over an arm of the river Nene.

From this point the walk goes across the meadows to look at the mill, returning later directly to this steel bridge.

Cross the bridge and then go over a stile beside a steel gate into a field. Walk beside the fence on the right and at the far side of the field cross a wooden footbridge over a wide ditch. Go straight ahead towards Water Newton Lock, crossing a small wooden bridge just before you get there. Go over the lock on a steel walkway beside the lifting lock gate and turn sharp left on a path which leads round to the front of Water Newton Mill, where you meet the end of a narrow road on the south side of the river Nene. Have a good look at the mill, now tastefully converted into a range of flower-decked cottages, in a picturesque riverside setting. If you have time, wander up the road to the tiny village of Water Newton. Retrace your steps on the same path, back to the large steel bridge over the Nene, which you crossed earlier.

Having re-crossed the bridge, turn right over a stile and keep alongside the river, following the waymarked Nene Way, a permissive path. In 50 yards cross a bridge and a stile. At the end of the next field is a boardwalk and stile on the river bank. Continue along the river bank and, at the next field boundary, go straight on, over a stile.

Follow the river on your right for about 250 yards, then just before some willow trees turn left, away from the river. In less than 100 yards you will come to the end of a channel of water on the right.

Keep beside the backwater as it bends round to the right. However, in just over 100 yards, and before passing some bushes on the right, turn half-left towards the wooden handrails of a footbridge you can just see, in line with a prominent lone poplar tree on rising ground ahead. Cross the bridge and climb up to cross a stile beside a gate in the corner of the field. Ahead, in the distance, is Alwalton church. Follow the fence on the left as it bends first left, then right. At the corner go over a stile onto a broad headland for 50 yards and then, after another stile, along a narrow footpath to a tarmac road.

Turn right and, in 50 yards, where the tarmac ends, turn left on a cart track and go through a small gate, keeping beside a hedge on the left. Pause to glance back at the Old Mill building. In another 100 yards, pass on the left the remains of an old tower windmill.

Bear right to cross Back Dyke on a long footbridge and then turn sharp left. Keep beside the river on the left for ¼ mile, where you will find a ford. Go a further 50 yards to cross a footbridge.

After re-crossing Back Dyke turn right beside the water. In a few yards turn left beside the river Nene on the right. Continue on the Nene Way along the bank of the Nene for about ½ mile, cross the Nene Valley Railway, and keep straight on beside the river. On the far side of the river Nene lie the extensive lakes of the Ferry Meadows Country Park.

About 300 yards beyond the railway turn left, over a stile or through a gate, into Landy Green Way, a broad grassy path. In ½ mile the path ends at a road. Turn right. At the T-junction turn left and walk into Castor and the start.

Other local attractions: The Nene Valley Railway is a private line running from Wansford (the station is just east of the A1) to Peterborough. The whole return journey is 15 miles. To obtain a timetable ring 01780 782854. During the year there are many special events, besides the scheduled runs. Thomas the Tank Engine sometimes pulls trains.

The walk passes within sight of Ferry Meadows Country Park. This comprises 500 acres of woods, meadows and lakes, with facilities for fishing, boating, horseriding, sailing, caravanning, camping, pitch and putt, nature walks and so on. Telephone: 01733 234443. The park is less than a mile from Castor, though the other side of the river. The Nene Valley Railway line has a station which serves Ferry Meadows Park.

④ Marholm
The Fitzwilliam Arms

Marholm has retained its rural charm despite being at the very edge of Peterborough. The village stands on an undulating limestone area to the north-west of the city and, like Barnack, many of its houses are built with the light brown local stone. St Mary's church with its 12th century tower stands somewhat isolated. Pedestrians use a pleasant tree-lined footpath but vehicles must take a cart track across a meadow to reach the church. The churchyard boundary is unusual, being a ditch, the church side of which is a vertical brick wall. This arrangement, known as a ha-ha, is more common in the vicinity of a stately home. Its purpose is to form a stock-proof boundary without causing any visible obstruction to the view. In the church are several memorials to members of the Fitzwilliam family.

The large and comfortable Fitzwilliam Arms comprises several eating and drinking areas, including a garden. Some of the beams have aphorisms inscribed on them, with which you may or may not agree. For instance, 'One barrel of wine can work more miracles than a church full of saints' and 'Where there is no wine love perishes'. Ranged around the rooms are high shelves crammed with old bottles, stone jars, stone hot water bottles, books and knick-knacks galore from times past. At the front of the pub is some topiary which has earned the pub the nickname of 'the Green Man'.

Culinary delights include rump, sirloin and T-bone steaks, tuna pasta bake, haddock fillets, sage and onion pork loin chops, grilled gammon steak topped with either fried egg or pineapple, and Cajun chicken. The marinaded turkey steaks, flavoured with blue cheese and sour cream, sound delicious, too. The 'Big Grill' is just that – a large mixed platter of steak, gammon, sausage, black pudding, lamb chop, fried egg, sauté mushrooms and deep-fried onion rings. In addition, there are vegetarian dishes, such as pasta shells and sweet corn with tomato and mozzarella cheese, broccoli and cream cheese bake, and leek and mushroom bake in a wholegrain mustard sauce. To follow, deep dish apple pie, hot pudding of the day, cheesecake, toffee pie, chocolate fudge cake, banana split and knickerbocker glory are there to tempt you. Children are welcome and a special menu is provided, but they are restricted to the large L-shaped area in the corner away from the bar – and they can play in the garden. A bottle and baby-food warming service is provided should your children be that young. Meals are served at lunchtimes and in the evenings seven days a week. The real ales served are Ansells, Tetley, Burton and a guest beer. There is also Olde English draught cider. Dogs are not welcome.

Telephone: 01733 262293.

How to get there: Marholm is on the western edge of Peterborough. From the A47 take the turning to Ailsworth and Castor. On the east side of Castor turn north for Marholm, which is reached in about 3 miles.

Parking: This presents no difficulties at the pub, and there are a few on-street spaces in Marholm.

Length of the walk: 4 miles. Map: OS Landranger sheet 142 Peterborough (inn GR 148021).

The walk passes the church and its ha-ha, and soon joins the route of the Torpel Way, an 11 mile walk from Stamford to Peterborough. Torpel is the name of a Norman manor which once covered a large part of the land in the locality. There was a castle, now demolished, and a manor house which was probably located at Helpston, and stood in a large medieval park.

The walk follows the Torpel Way through Burmer Wood, an ancient wood, and past Foster's Coppice. Leaving the path to Stamford, the route returns via Hayes Wood passing Pellett Hall, a farm, via minor roads, back to Marholm.

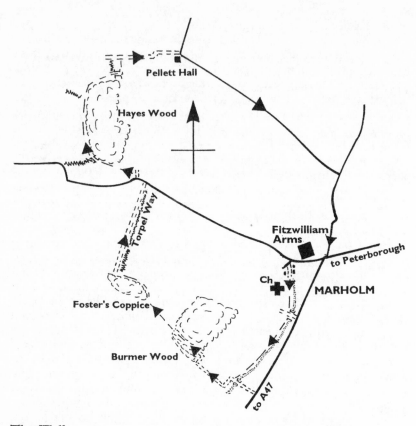

The Walk

From the Fitzwilliam Arms go right along the road and turn left into Church Walk. In 20 yards go left again, on a surfaced road leading to the church. Pass several large houses, some with a small stream meandering through the gardens. In a few yards, when the surfaced road ends, keep straight on along a path between mature trees as far as the entrance to the churchyard near a huge cedar tree.

Do not enter the churchyard but go through a kissing-gate beside the church wall and the ha-ha, into a field. Bear slightly left across a meadow and you will meet, at right angles, a farm track. Go to the point where the farm track crosses the stream by a narrow cart bridge, then walk beside the stream on your left. Cross a stile and continue on a broad headland beside the stream. The walk has joined the Torpel Way. In 300 yards a bridleway comes in from the left and, just after, there is a copse on the left.

At the corner, just beyond where the copse on the left ends, turn right on the bridleway, away from the stream with a very small hedge on the left, towards the edge of a wood. Turn right beside the trees for 50 yards and then, at a waymark, enter Burmer Wood on a broad bridleway. It is a lovely mature wood, mainly ash, but with sycamore, lime, sweet chestnut and oak. On leaving the wood go straight ahead on a grassy cart track towards the middle of Foster's Coppice, the trees ahead.

Pause and look round, because you are on a small hill with views on all sides. It is an interesting landscape with small woods and many isolated mature trees. When you reach Foster's Coppice the path leads you around it, skirting it on your left. Halfway along the side of the wood you come to a farm track at right angles. Here turn right along the Torpel Way – this section, from here to the road, is a permissive path.

In the unlikely event of the permissive section of the Torpel Way being closed, you should continue straight ahead along the public bridleway.

Follow the Torpel Way beside a thorn hedge, on the right, across the field to the road and go left. Where the road bends round to the left, go right, through an iron gateway on a farm track, and in 20 yards go left over a stile, which is inscribed 'Torpel Way 1987', into a meadow. Pass to the left of the first oak tree and then continue parallel to the hedge on the right. Go through the bridlegate and continue with woodland on the right. About 20 yards beyond the corner of the woodland go right through a bridlegate and across a bridge over a ditch into a large field. Turn right along a headland, with Hayes Wood on the right. At a field boundary go straight on, still following the wood on the right. Pass through a gap in a cross-hedge and still continue with the wood to the right. The path is gradually bending round to the right.

At the hedge which is at the corner of Hayes Wood, go straight on, over a bridge constructed by the Peterborough Community Programme in 1986, and immediately turn left on a broad grassy headland path, following a hedge and ditch on the left. This path leads out to a gravel farm drive. Go right. In about ¼ mile the farm drive reaches a road at a bend. Go straight on along the quiet road for about a mile. There are fairly wide verges on both sides.

At the T-junction go right and in about 300 yards go over a bridge to enter Marholm. In a further 300 yards, at a staggered junction, turn right towards Barnack and Ufford, to the Fitzwilliam Arms.

5 Grafham
The Montagu Arms

Grafham is a small village at the edge of Grafham Water, an attractive lake where sailing, fishing and other water-based recreational activities occur. In the early 1960s, however, there was no lake and the lives of the local residents must have been drastically changed by the construction of the dam across the valley and the formation of Grafham Water. Completed in 1966, it is a huge lake about 3 miles long and 1¼ miles wide, covering 15,600 acres and holding 13 billion gallons of water. It is the second largest of a group of five interconnected storage reservoirs which provide the water for the 1.5 million people who live in and around Bedfordshire and Northamptonshire. The reservoir is kept replenished by pumping, in winter, water from the river Great Ouse. Now the reservoir has an additional use as a leisure and recreational resource. People visit the lake for its beauty and to observe the wildlife. There are cycle trails around the edge and bikes can be hired at the visitors' centre.

The Montagu Arms in Grafham village was built on the old railway sidings, with what was the old railway station next door. It is a very popular pub. The atmosphere is friendly and the food good and plentiful. A large log fire burns on colder days. There are bar games in the public bar, and upholstered chairs and benches in the lounge bar. Outside there is a well-equipped children's play area, and a barbecue. Live entertainment is regularly arranged during the summer. Some overnight accommodation is also available. The restaurant section, serving a traditional Sunday lunch, was fully booked on a chill day in March; nevertheless there was plenty of food and room for eating available in the rest of the pub. Booking might be advisable, though it is by no means necessary.

The menu is quite mouth-watering. How about black tiger prawns, or home-made soup to start, then 8 oz rump steak, an 8 oz gammon steak with egg or pineapple, a 14 oz mixed grill, steak diane or chasseur or au poivre, a very large Grafham trout, chicken Kiev or chicken curry? Hot 'n' spicy or lemon spiced butterfly chicken breasts with chips or hash browns are delicious, or then again you could try an 8 oz salmon steak in white wine and prawn sauce. Besides peach melba, ices and gâteaux, there are such old favourites as chocolate sponge, treacle pudding or spotted dick, all with custard. Meals are served at lunchtime and in the evenings seven days a week. On summer Saturdays the pub remains open all day. The real ales served are Greene King, Bass and one guest beer. Red Rock draught cider is on sale, too. Well-behaved dogs may go in the public bar.

Telephone: 01480 810071.

How to get there: Grafham is about 6 miles north-west of St Neots. It can be reached from the A14 west of Huntingdon. Take the turn to Ellington, 2 miles west of the interchange with the A1, and continue southwards for 2 miles to Grafham. The Montagu Arms is in the centre of the village.

Parking: Parking is available at the Montagu Arms. In addition, there is a large car park beside the Grafham Water visitors' centre about a mile south of the village.

Length of the walk: 4 miles, or 5 miles if you want to include the visitors' centre (an extra ½ mile each way). Map: OS Landranger sheet 153 Bedford, Huntingdon and surrounding area (inn GR 161693).

Grafham Water lies in a shallow valley. The walk climbs gently out of the valley, crosses a ridge and descends a short distance towards the village of Ellington. The path skirts the woodland on the side of a hill and then the route joins the Three Shires Way, a 37 mile bridleway which starts beside Grafham Water and, after running through Northamptonshire, ends in Buckinghamshire, in the Salcey Forest.

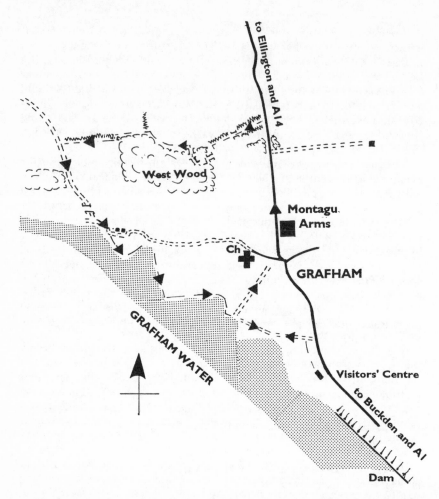

The walk returns over the hill to the shore of Grafham Water and continues alongside the lake. You can choose to extend the route to the Anglian Water visitors' centre, if you wish.

The Walk

From the Montagu Arms turn right, away from the village, along the road towards Ellington. In ½ mile, at the top of the hill, pass on the right a tarmac farm road leading to Redwood Lodge. Continue on, down the hill, passing woods on both sides. When the wood on the left ends, continue past a field on the left and immediately after that field turn left, over a sleeper bridge into a lovely green lane, being a narrow grass path between hedges. Come to a substantial bridge over a ditch. Keep straight on, with a hedge on the right and a field on the left.

At the end of the field go left for about 20 yards and cross another substantial bridge, into the wood. After the bridge go left for about 30 yards, and then go right. From here the route veers to the right and you will soon be leaving the trees. Do not be tempted to take minor ways to the left which lead deeper into the wood. Soon cross another substantial sleeper bridge after which you bear round a little more to the right to come to a similar bridge at the edge of the trees.

Cross the bridge and turn left on a grassy headland path, following along the edge of the woods, with primroses in the springtime. At a corner of the woods, go through a cross-hedge and continue on this wide grassy headland, with the woodland on the left.

Half-right you can see, apparently close together, the spires of Easton and Spaldwick churches. Just beyond the end of the wood go left over a broad culvert and then right and follow the hedge on the right. In the far corner of the field go through a hedge to reach a green lane known as Hartham Street, an ancient road from Easton to Grafham, which is now part of the Three Shires Way. Turn left along the green lane which skirts Culpher Wood. After leaving the wood swing slightly left and then right to go under a former railway bridge and see Grafham Water ahead. On reaching the water's edge go left on a gravel road.

Where the road bends left past some buildings keep straight on beside the water, on a grass footpath. There is a gate and No horses sign. On the right in the lake is the aeration tower. Keep beside the lake, on a permissive path. Soon you will be walking towards Grafham and seeing the church spire a few degrees to your left. On reaching a small bay turn right beside the lake. Now you are walking almost away from the church. At the next headland you come to a gate and the end of the tarmac road which leads to the village.

To go the visitors' centre, do not go through the gate but turn right along a gravel cycle track. Keep on the same gravel track which will lead you to the Anglian Water car park and visitors' centre. On your return, retrace your steps to the gate at the end of the tarmac road.

Walk straight up the road, pass a pair of cottages and later some barns on the right. At a T-junction, where the cycle route goes left towards the church, from Church Hill, turn right and then go left to the Montagu Arms, along Breach Road.

6 Stilton
The Bell Inn

To most people the name 'Stilton' is synonymous with cheese, but the famous cheese was never made here. Its wide success was due to the marketing skill of an enterprising landlord of the Bell Inn. The cheese was actually made just south of Melton Mowbray, by a housekeeper at Quenby Hall, who supplied the cheese to her brother-in-law, Cooper Thornhill, the landlord of the Bell for almost 30 years. He was a great character who was full of ideas for promoting his business, and he made the excellent cheese famous.

This is a most inviting, intriguing inn, dating back to 1500 and possibly earlier. It is essentially in two bits, the hotel section, and the part known as the Village Bar, separated by the great courtyard, where the coaches used to arrive and where now large plate glass doors close this off from the broad street. The sumptuous hotel has two rooms with four-poster beds. The Village Bar is comfortable and welcoming.

There is a wide choice of delicious meals – lamb casseroled in cider and rosemary with Stilton dumplings, taco shells filled with cumin and chilli spiced minced beef, chicken Mexicana with pilau rice, and two-fillet stir-fry, pork and beef, in a black bean sauce, to name but a few. There are vegetarian dishes on offer, too. On ordering your food at the bar you are given a wooden 'bell' with a number on it, which you take to your table. The waitress then looks around and matches your meal to your bell. The pub is open and meals are served at the usual times. Tetley, Ruddles County, Marston's Pedigree Bitter and a guest ale are on sale, as is Old English draught cider.

Telephone: 01733 245066.

How to get there: Stilton is just off the A1, south-west of Peterborough. From Cambridge and the south, go to Huntingdon and continue on the A14 to join the A1 at Alconbury. The turning to Stilton is 8 miles further north. The Bell is on the Great North Road, in the middle of the village. From the north, on the A1, turn off to Stilton, ¼ mile south of the Norman Cross roundabout.

Parking: The road through the village is wide and there is plenty of parking space on both sides of the road. In addition, you will find a large car park at the rear of The Bell.

Length of the walk: 4½ miles. Map: OS Landranger sheet 142 Peterborough (inn GR 162893).

To the west of Stilton there are a number of settlements nestling in shallow valleys in an area of mixed farming. This short walk takes in the 3 small villages of Folksworth, Caldecote and Denton. It is a fairly easy route but at times it can be muddy, so go well shod. Although not particularly hilly, between Denton and Stilton the walk reaches a high point where there is a good view stretching across towards Peterborough and the edge of the fens.

The Walk

From the Bell, cross the road and go up Church Street, almost opposite. Pass St Mary Magdalene's church and soon follow the road as it makes a sharp bend to the right. In 100 yards turn left along Caldecote Road, signed to 'Caldecote and Folksworth'. Just after the last house on the right and where the road bends left, leave the road at a footpath sign at a gate and cross the field diagonally to a stile at the opposite corner, passing a small pond on the way.

Cross the next field, going towards a radio tower in the distance. On the far side, take a path between wooden fences, cross a stile and reach a housing estate. Cross the road and go straight on along Blackmans Road. Where Hawthorne Road bears right, take the footpath straight on and shortly reach a road.

Bear right along the road and at the T-junction, where the main traffic goes right, turn left along Manor Road. A sign says 'Folksworth only'. Opposite the Fox public house on the right, bear left into Elm Road, which, after passing the former village school, turns left.

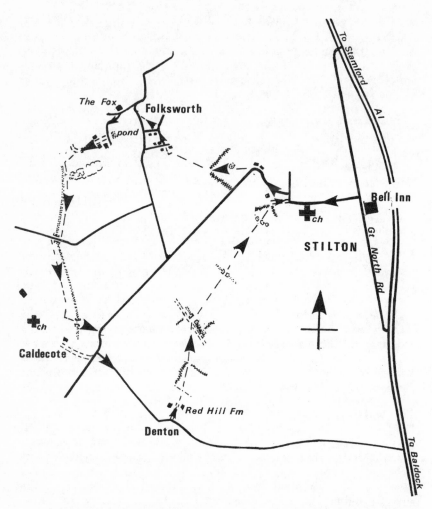

On the left you will soon reach the small village pond. There is a seat here and a notice requesting people not to feed the ducks. Opposite the pond, at a bridleway sign, turn right along a farm track. Go straight through the farmyard, between barns and through a gate. Keep on the farm track until it starts to bend to the right. Go through a small pedestrian gate on the left and cross the pasture to a gate displaying a waymark.

Beyond the gate, keep straight on for about 50 yards and at the end of a shallow ditch, close beside a post bearing waymarks, turn left alongside the ditch on the right and go through a pedestrian gate into a large arable field. Walk the headland path, with a stream on the right, until you reach a road. Go right for 40 yards and, at the footpath sign, turn left over a stile and cross the small meadow to another stile. Keep straight on, parallel to the stream on the left. You can see, on the right, Caldecote Manor Farm with its strange-looking central tower, and, a little further on, the church with a tiny belfry.

Cross a third stile and bear slightly right towards the right-hand side of some buildings. On reaching a tree in the centre of the field swing half-left and, after crossing a culvert over the stream and two stiles, reach a road. Turn right for 100 yards and take the minor road on the left to 'Denton'. In ¼ mile, having passed an old thatched white cottage on the left, at a junction, follow the road round to the left, and in about 200 yards where the road veers round to the right, and close to a ruined church, just visible among the trees on the right, take the tarmac farm road on the left.

Go straight across the farmyard of Red Hill Farm and through a gate into a small field, on the far side of which an iron gate leads into a larger pasture. Climb to a stile in the top left-hand corner of the field which leads into an arable field. Bear slightly left, going towards the right side of two trees which appear close together, and you will reach the corner of the field.

Cross a cart track at right angles and go over a culvert into the next, a very large, field. If the path ahead is not clear to see, continue across the field in the same direction as the hedge behind you. In about 50 yards you will be at the top of the hill and the route will be clearer. Straight ahead, in front of a group of tall chimneys in the distance, is the tower of Yaxley church. Your direction is a little to the left of the tower. Go to a gap in the hedge and over a two-sleeper bridge.

At first go in the same direction as before, towards the left-hand end of the houses of Stilton. In the middle of the field, change direction slightly and make towards a point in a line of poplars about 50 yards to the left of Stilton church tower. At the poplars, cross a stile and then walk over a meadow to the opposite corner and go out through a narrow gate. Bear right along a lane which leads into a tarmac road.

In a few yards join Church Street and go straight on past the church, back to the Bell Inn.

Other local attractions: Holme Fen Posts. To get there from Stilton, go north along the A1 as far as the Norman Cross roundabout, make a U-turn and go south on the A1 for 3 miles. Turn left on the B660 for Holme. Immediately before the railway crossing turn left and in ½ mile turn right and shortly cross the railway. Continue on the road through the woods for about ½ mile. The posts are on the right, just off the road and beyond a drainage ditch. There is a small layby opposite the footbridge leading to the posts (GR 203894).

7 Abbots Ripton
The Three Horseshoes

Abbots Ripton and its neighbour, Kings Ripton, are a pair of tiny rural villages in a shallow valley about 5 miles from the edge of the Cambridgeshire fens. In both villages a few dwellings nestle around the church. Abbots Ripton Hall is a prominent building, not regularly open to the public, and just south of the village stands a large modern village hall. The 2 mile long main runway of Alconbury airfield is just a mile away, and planes may be seen and heard on days when flying takes place.

The 400 year old Three Horseshoes, with its very distinctively patterned thatched roof, lies at a road junction in the centre of the village, close to the church. Note that the ridge of the thatched cottage opposite is surmounted by a straw bird, the thatcher's trademark. The taller than average customer needs to watch his head when entering this pub from the front as the old beams in the front bar are quite low. In winter two cheery, blazing log fires burn in the bars. This is a very comfortable pub and the food is plentiful. The walls are adorned with all manner of bits of harness, both leather and brass. There are also old guns and swords. Besides the bars, with their many tables and upholstered seats, there is a small restaurant. Children can play in the garden, and eat with their parents in the family room.

Fish – scampi, lemon sole, trout, plaice – is available, as well as vegetarian dishes, various interesting platters and a selection of hot and cold sweets. Much of the food is home-made. Meals are served each lunchtime and evening, with the exception of Monday evenings. The real ales on offer are Courage Directors and John Smith's. The pub also serves Dry Blackthorn draught cider. Dogs are not allowed on the premises.

Telephone: 014873 440.

How to get there: Abbots Ripton is about 3 miles north of Huntingdon. From the north, use the A1, and then, just south of Sawtry, take the B1090 towards St Ives. The Three Horseshoes is reached in about 3 miles. From other directions, turn off the A141 north of Huntingdon on a minor road to Abbots Ripton.

Parking: The pub's car park is large.

Length of the walk: 4½ miles. Map: OS Landranger sheet 142 Peterborough (inn GR 232779).

At first the walk crosses meadows to Abbots Ripton Hall. It continues along a good farm road, skirting Wennington Wood, and then along a minor road towards Little Raveley. The route goes along a green lane known as The Butts, possibly the place where, in Tudor times, villagers had their compulsory archery practice. The return is along a cross-field path to the hamlet of Wennington, passing a small pond, then along a minor road, back to the start.

The Walk

Come out of the Three Horseshoes and go left along a minor road, passing some thatched cottages. In 150 yards, where the tarmac road snakes left and right to a pair of white cottages, go straight ahead through a pedestrian gate into a pasture, and follow the hedge on the left.

Over to the right, beyond the road, you can see the magnificent modern village hall cum sports pavilion, whilst on the left, behind tall trees is a large moated house. Where the hedge you have been following turns left, keep straight on across the field to the hedge opposite, to find and cross a long timber bridge, then go through a kissing-gate and across a short timber bridge.

Cross a tarmac track at right angles and go through a pedestrian gate on a narrow footpath through a small belt of trees, to leave the trees by another pedestrian gate. From this point the map shows the right of way going straight across the field to a field gate 50 yards to the left of

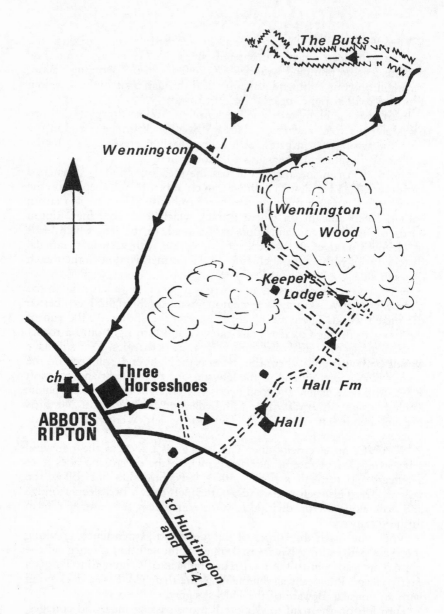

The Butts

Wennington

Wennington
Wood

Keepers
Lodge

ch

Three
Horseshoes

ABBOTS
RIPTON

Hall Fm

Hall

to Huntingdon
and A 141

the cottage on the opposite side of the field. However, people seem to have skirted round the field, by walking half-right to the garden fence on the right and then following the edge of the field (fence on the right) until a concrete farm track is reached.

34

Turn left on to the farm track and in 100 yards go right through the five-bar gate seen when you entered this field. Go across a meadow towards a green pumping station. Skirt the fence of the pumping station, leaving it on your right, and leave the field through a kissing-gate to join a tarmac road at right angles.

In front is the high buttressed brick wall of Abbots Ripton Hall. Turn left along the road and cross a stream by a brick bridge. Pass on the right the wrought iron gates, with a heraldic lion crest, leading to the hall. In spring there are masses of daffodils here.

Shortly you can see, half-left across the meadow, the large, thatched farmhouse, Hall Farm, with a brown-red colourwash. Still keeping on the tarmac road, pass on the right another farmhouse. This one is a cream colour. Keep straight on where a track which leads to Kings Ripton heads off to the right, and soon pass a road, to the left, which leads to Keeper's Lodge, an unusual looking house with a steep pyramidal thatched roof with a central chimney and a dormer window in the thatch on each side.

When you reach the wood at a three-way junction go left, still on the tarmac farm drive, skirting Wennington Wood on the right. Keep beside the mixed wood. There are bluebells here in the spring. At the end of the trees go through a large brick gateway and turn right onto a road.

Walk along the quiet road with verges on both sides. You still have woods on your right. Where the trees on the right end, still keep on the road, which makes a bend to the left and one to the right and goes left again. And now, where the road bends sharply right go left at the public bridleway sign, on a grassy lane with hedges on both sides. In 200 yards the lane bends left. You can see, over to the left, Wennington Woods where you were before.

Go under an electricity line. The lane gives a kick to the right and then swings left. Pause at a waymark, where the green lane goes over a culvert and through a hedge into a large field. Do not follow the waymark but, just before the culvert, turn left over a two-sleeper bridge and walk along a crop division towards some trees surrounding a farm in the distance.

When you reach the corner of the farmstead garden fence, go along the grass path, with a hawthorn hedge on the left and a fence on the right. This leads out to the road. Turn right into Wennington. This is a pretty village. Practically all the buildings are thatched. Pass a duck-pond with an unusual 'Beware of the Ducks' sign.

Turn left on the road to Abbots Ripton, passing more old cottages, one of which has a similar thatching pattern to that of the Three Horseshoes. Walk along the wide grass verge back to the start.

Godmanchester
The Black Bull

8

The towns of Huntingdon and Godmanchester lie close together, but separated by the river Great Ouse. Before 1973, Huntingdon was the county town of Huntingdonshire. It owes its importance, at least in part, to the 13th century bridge over the Ouse. The Roman road from the North, Ermine Street, crossed the river near this point, on its way to a settlement at Godmanchester and then south towards London. Just by the bridge are the remains of Huntingdon Castle, a motte and bailey which must have dominated the river valley.

The Black Bull is at the northern end of Godmanchester. It stands on what used to be the main London to Scotland road, and in the 1800s the inn was a coach staging post. Now it is a popular local pub. Parts of the building are over 300 years old. The large lounge, for both eating and drinking, is subdivided, by such features as the huge fireplace and the change in level, into small intimate areas which, together with the settles, give the whole pub a cosy atmosphere.

The menu is wide-ranging, and the food is good and plentiful. Dishes such as pork fillet chasseur, peppered rump steak, Cajun prawns with salad, mixed grill, sirloin and T-bone steaks, spicy chicken wings with a dip or an enormous Yorkie filled with savoury mince can be followed by treacle pudding, spotted dick and custard, apple pie, Death-by-Chocolate, apple and blackberry strudel, brandy baskets or chocolate profiteroles and a selection of cold sweets. The real ales available are Flowers Original, Shefford Bitter and Wethered. Strongbow draught cider is also on offer. Children are well catered for as there is a family room and a garden area for them to play in. As food is served in all parts of the pub dogs are not permitted (except guide dogs).

The pub is open and food is served seven days a week, from 11 am to 2.30 pm and 6 pm to 11 pm on Mondays to Fridays, with a later lunch closing of 3 pm on Saturdays. The Sunday hours are from 11 am to 3 pm and 7.30 pm to 10.30 pm.

Telephone 01480 453310.

How to get there: From the A14 dual-carriageway, exit at the interchange just south of Huntingdon. Follow signs for Godmanchester and Huntingdon. The Black Bull is on the right at the far side of Godmanchester.

Parking: There is ample parking behind the Black Bull, and it is possible to park along the street.

Length of the walk: 3 miles. Map: OS Landranger sheet 153 Bedford, Huntingdon and surrounding area (inn GR 244709).

This easy walk from Godmanchester crosses the river Great Ouse, which forms the western boundary of Godmanchester, and then circles a vast common, Port Holme, which can be wet at times. At one time Huntingdon Racecourse was here, and in the First World War it was a training airfield. Now it is sensitively managed, a designated Site of Special Scientific Interest, where snake's-head fritillaries and cowslips grow.

Beyond the common, and after crossing another arm of the river, the walk enters Huntingdon, going as far as the church and the old grammar school where Oliver Cromwell and Samuel Pepys were educated. Allow extra time to explore the town centre, if you can. The return is down the High Street and across a new footbridge beside the ancient 13th century stone roadbridge, to Godmanchester. The old bridge has many recesses on each side into which pedestrians could go to avoid the passing horses.

The Walk

Leave the Black Bull, going south, left, towards the town centre of Godmanchester. In about 300 yards, opposite the Rose and Crown Quaker Centre, go right into Mill Yard and cross a couple of sluices to the other side of the river.

Follow the river on your left, passing a children's play area on the

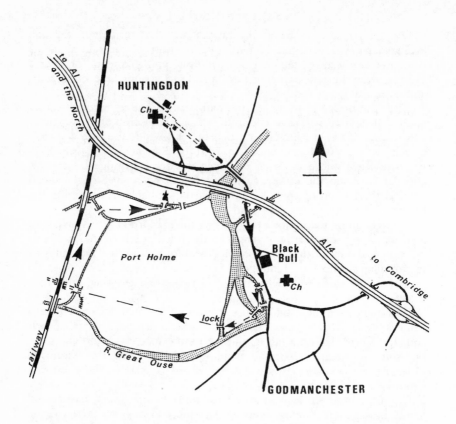

right, until you reach an elegant, white, wooden footbridge. This is the Chinese Bridge, originally built in 1827 and replaced by a replica in 1960 by Godmanchester Borough Council. Continue past the bridge and cross a stretch of water by a bridge and weir, with water rushing towards Huntingdon.

Keep on with the fast-flowing river on your left. Cross two wooden footbridges, bearing 'Ouse Valley Way' signs and continue on over a lock by means of a concrete bridge. You are now on the 225 acre Port Holme common. This is part of the flood plain of the river Great Ouse. Away in the distance on the far side of the meadow you can see a reddish-painted steel railway bridge, which carries the railway over the river. You head to the right of that bridge. When you get nearer to the railway, the way will become clearer to see. You are making for a narrow lane which leads to a brick-arch railway bridge. When at the far side of the meadow go through a metal kissing-gate, over a brick cartbridge, into the lane towards the railway.

Do not go quite as far as the railway arch but turn right, through a dilapidated wooden gate about 50 yards short of the railway. Walk through the meadow, parallel to the railway embankment, for over a ¼ mile, near the end swinging right a little to go up three brick steps and over a wooden footbridge.

After the bridge go right, on the path that meanders through scrub, some 7 ft high at first, then continue through low scrub until eventually you reach a wooden gate. Go through the gap beside the gate and over a weir with a sluice gate, made in 1931 by Ransomes and Rapier in Ipswich. In 50 more yards go left over another cartbridge by a sluice and climb on up the farm lane to join a narrow road. Straight ahead beyond the garden of the large house is the embankment carrying the hurtling traffic along the A14 road.

Go right along the minor road, passing the Edward House Trust, with a crown atop three narrow lozenges in the brick porch of the house, to a T-junction. Go left under the road. Ahead of you, across two lanes of fast-moving traffic, lies Huntingdon. You could wait all day to cross, so go left for 80 yards to a light-controlled pedestrian crossing, and cross in safety.

Bear right past the coach station towards the green and go left into Princes Street. This will take you to the Market Square, All Saints' church and the Town Hall opposite it, and across the road from the church is the solid four-square Norman building which is now the Cromwell Museum, for you are, as the Tourist Board proclaims, 'in Cromwell Country'.

From the museum turn south-east along the High Street, passing All Saints Passage and Literary Walk to the stub end of High Street. Carry on in the same direction, with great care, to cross Castle Moat Road. On your right you can see the remains of the old castle on Castle Hills, topped now by an Armada Beacon basket. Keep on, past the Old Bridge Hotel on your right, and then for safety's sake take the modern footbridge beside the narrow, old stone road bridge over the river Great Ouse, and go on under the A14 road and into lime tree lined Post Street, back into Godmanchester and the Black Bull.

Other local attractions: The Cromwell Museum in the Market Place in Huntingdon is open from April to October from 11 am to 1 pm and 2 pm to 5 pm on Tuesdays to Fridays, and 11 am to 1 pm and 2 pm to 4 pm at weekends. From November to March the hours are 1 pm to 4 pm on Tuesdays to Fridays and 11 am to 1 pm and 2 pm to 4 pm on Saturdays and 2 pm to 4 pm on Sundays. It is closed on bank holidays, except Good Friday. It houses portraits of Oliver Cromwell and his family, coins, medals and memorabilia belonging to Oliver Cromwell. Admission is free, but donations are appreciated.

⑨ Graveley
The Three Horseshoes

This area is a plateau with a few streams carving shallow valleys in it. The villages of Graveley, Yelling and Papworth St Agnes have grown up around the streams. Graveley, an attractive little place, cares even about the appearance of its bus shelters, which in hexagonal shape and style are quite distinctive, adding to the street scene. In the High Street, by the Toseland Road, is a Tudor cottage with a jettied upper storey. Yelling, its dwellings clustered along the road, lies on both sides of its small valley. The church stands high on the eastern side. Papworth St Agnes, just west of the old Roman road, Ermine Street, is a tiny settlement which is isolated by being at the end of a cul-de-sac off the road to Graveley. On a small grassy island in the centre of the village stands a square brick building which was once a communal bakery.

The Three Horseshoes is immaculate and very comfortable. The bar runs from the front right through to the back, with access from the car park. Upholstered benches line the walls and there are many small tables. At the bar are comfortable, unusual swivel bar stools with backs to them. Leading off the bar is a well-appointed restaurant, which is open in the evenings (booking advised). Old county maps adorn the walls and a row of tankards hang from a beam.

Healthy meals, low in fat and mostly home-cooked, are featured on the menu and on offer are 16 oz T-bone steaks, 8 oz sirloin or rump steaks, tagliatelle carbonara or au salmon, peppered mackerel, beef Stroganov, chicken chasseur, chicken curry and roast chicken, beef and Guinness pie, grilled halibut and trout, and chef's stir-fry with pork, pineapple, ginger and fried rice. Such vegetarian dishes as lasagne, moussaka, mushroom Stroganov, vegetable curry or vegetable chilli are also available. Round the meal off with banana split, banana flambé, pineapple in kirsch or crêpes suzettes. Meals are served at lunchtimes and in the evenings every day of the week. Such real ales as Ruddles and Marston's Pedigree Bitter are offered, and Strongbow draught cider. In the interest of hygiene dogs are not welcome.

Telephone: 01480 830992.

How to get there: Graveley is 6 miles south of Huntingdon and is reached from the A1198 Huntingdon to Royston road. From the Caxton Gibbet roundabout on the A428 west of Cambridge, head northwards for 3½ miles, turning left to reach Graveley in 2 miles. The Three Horseshoes is in the main street in the village.

Parking: There is plenty of parking behind the pub and quite a bit of street-side parking in the village.

Length of the walk: 4½ miles. Map: OS Landranger sheet 153 Bedford, Huntingdon and surrounding area (inn GR 248640).

This triangular walk goes from Graveley along a green lane and then rises to Yelling, where it descends to cross a small stream, rising thereafter to the church. The walk continues along a road past the next shallow valley. The route to Papworth St Agnes is along a ridge with good views and the return to Graveley is across farmland.

The Walk

From the Three Horseshoes go left along the village street, which soon makes a sharp left bend. In about ¼ mile, at Home Farm, go right on the tarmac road, signed 'Public Bridleway Yelling ¾'. In about 50 yards, where the tarmac ends, continue on a grassy track down a hill. At the bottom turn left at the waymark and go on along a grassy path, with a little rivulet on the right. Shortly, the path swings round to the right and crosses the stream. Leave the stream and gradually climb out of the valley along a hollow lane which ends near the top of the hill.

Pause here and look over to the east, where you can see a wide view of farmland and the fens beyond. Looking ahead, across a field, you can see the houses at Yelling.

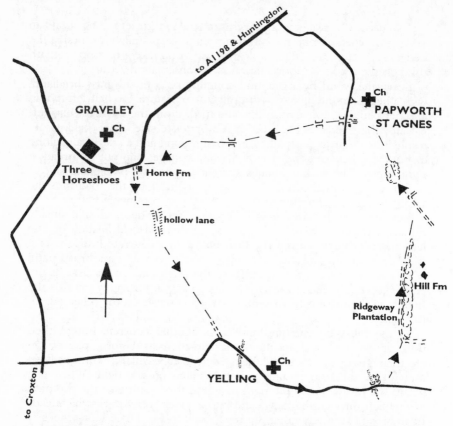

Continue on a narrower bridleway, with a ditch on the right and a hedge on the left. Go down a slight valley, then climb again up to a lane called Bridle End, leading to the village of Yelling. Pass some cottages and a white house on the left and a thatched white house on the right. Go left along the road, passing the village sign, down the hill. At the bottom cross a bridge with white railings and climb up the village street, passing Yelling church on your left.

Keep on the road for ½ mile to where, after dropping into a shallow valley, you cross a small stream beside a little copse on the left. The road climbs again and at the next field boundary on the left, go left at a Ramblers' Association waymark, over a concrete bridge to a broad headland path towards the woods ahead.

Bear slightly left at the wood, on a hard farm track, to skirt the edge of Ridgeway Plantation. Where the track turns right to the fruit farm, Hill Farm, go straight ahead on a grassy headland. At the end of the plantation, keep on in the same direction. This is a high point with wide views ahead. On reaching a gravel farm track, turn left along it and in 100 yards, where the farm road swings right, keep straight on beside the hedge. At the corner of a wood, by a waymark, take a narrow footpath through the wood. A notice says it is a Conservation Area.

Leave the wood by a gate and continue on a broad grass headland, with a hedge on the right. Cross a stile into a pasture. Go half-left to join another path at a waymark within the field. From the waymark turn left towards the middle of the trees at the opposite side of the field. Cross a stile into a narrow footpath, going past a pond and a stream and along a short lane between two thatched white cottages and out to a road at right angles. The walk continues straight on across a bridge and stile.

However, from this point you can go right along the road into the village to see the church and the old Victorian communal bakery.

Returning to the circular walk, go over the bridge and stile already mentioned, into a pasture. Keep close to the mid-field bushes, on the left, and on the far side of the field find a long concrete bridge over a wide deep stream and then continue in the next field on a broad path, with a deep ditch on the left. Where the ditch ends, walk straight on. At the top of the hill a waymark points straight on, roughly towards the middle of the three pairs of semi-detached cottages on the other side of the valley.

In the valley bottom find and cross another concrete bridge, then walk across the field in the same direction as before, passing an electricity pole to reach the field edge at a waymark. Turn half-left and follow the field boundary, with a ditch on the right. When you get to the hedge, go to the right of it and then soon take the footpath slightly left through the hedge and into a wider grassy track which leads to the road. Turn left along the road, back to the Three Horseshoes.

10 Waresley
The Duncombe Arms

Waresley, Great and Little Gransden, Abbotsley and Gamblingay are a group of villages, relatively close together, near the border with Bedfordshire. Like much of the south-western side of Cambridgeshire, this is rolling agricultural countryside drained by small streams flowing in shallow valleys. Between Waresley and Great Gransden lies a large area of woodland, ¾ mile long and ¼ mile wide, which comprises Waresley Wood and Gransden Wood, most of which is a nature reserve where wild flowers abound.

The Duncombe Arms is a charming pub with a very relaxing atmosphere. The comfortable lounge is set out with tables and chairs beside the many windows which look out over the village. Alongside the rear wall are easy chairs with some tables for those who maybe are not having a meal. At the end of the room is a french door leading out to a garden. A fire burns cheerily in the large grate, on cool days. To the rear of the main rooms is a family room. The restaurant, to the right of the front door, is resplendent in pink and white napery.

There is a wide menu to choose from. Venison hotpot, rogan josh, chicken tikka, broccoli Provençal, spare ribs or seafood platter are a few of the main courses, with sticky toffee meringue, apple strudel, 'lovable lemon lush' and other sweets to follow. Coffee, accompanied by a jug of cream rather than mini plastic pots of the UHT version, completes the meal. Food is served both at lunchtimes and in the evenings, seven days a week. Greene King real ales are on offer, as is Blackthorn draught cider. Dogs are not permitted in the pub.

Telephone: 01767 650265.

How to get there: Waresley is 12 miles west of Cambridge. From the A428 St Neots to Cambridge road, turn south at Eltisley on the B1040. You reach Waresley in 3 miles. The pub is opposite the church, in the centre of the village.

Parking: You will find plenty of parking space on the corner forecourt, and more behind the pub.

Length of the walk: 4½ miles. Allow extra time to explore the woods, if you can. Map: OS Landranger sheet 153 Bedford, Huntingdon and surrounding area (inn GR 250546).

This circular walk to the Gransdens follows, at first, a cart track across a small ridge with good views of the area, passing close to a small private airfield. The path then descends slowly beside a small watercourse, passing Waresley Wood, a nature reserve belonging to the Bedfordshire and Huntingdonshire Naturalists Trust, and, skirting Little Gransden, continues to the village of Great Gransden, in the valley. St Bartholomew's church stands prominently above the village. The return is across pasture and along the western edge of Waresley Wood, with a short diversion within it.

The Walk

Leave the Duncombe Arms, crossing the Gamlingay road, to go along Vicarage Road, a 'No Through Road', opposite. There are some lovely thatched cottages along here. On the left is the old Victorian vicarage. When the road ends, at Chase Farm, carry on past the house on the left and the new farm buildings, on the 'Public Bridleway'. It is a wide cart track crossing a large field with fine distant views from this high land. The track continues for just over ½ mile and then you pass a cross-hedge on the right. There is a waymark indicating a footpath to the right here. Continue straight on for about 80 yards, with a ditch on the left. Bear left on the cart track, following the ditch, now a small stream, on the left. Soon you reach a point where a wide grass lane goes off to the right.

Here the official route of the bridleway you are following goes right a few yards and then continues in the same direction as before, along

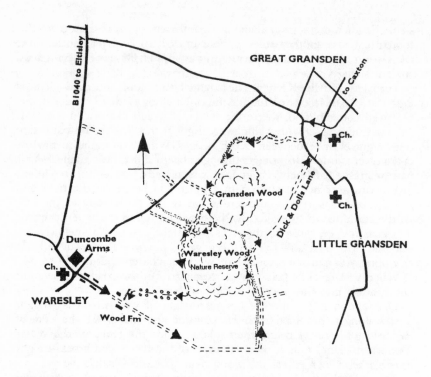

the edge of the field for about 400 yards.

Alternatively, make a short diversion through the edge of Waresley Wood, which is open to the public. From the place where the wide track goes right, cross the stream on the left by a wide culvert, and then swing right to continue in the same direction as before but now with the stream on your right. In just over 100 yards you reach the wood. Keep straight on, with the stream a few yards away on the right. Just after passing the path into Waresley Wood, cross the stream again and follow the broad grassy headland path, with woods on the left. Go through a cross-hedge and carry on as before, on the wide bridleway.

Half-right you can see the tower of Little Gransden church, and further to the right the arms of a distant windmill. Keep on beside the hedge which marks the edge of the woods. Go through a cross-hedge and into a narrow path between a paddock on right and a hedge on left. Ahead is the tower, surmounted by a spire, of Great Gransden church.

Later you walk in a lane with hedges on both sides, and come out to a road. Go 10 yards to the right on the road and then left over a stile and walk towards the church. Swing left a little, following the hedge on the left. Pass through a wooden gate, going over a stream and crossing a stile beside a metal gate. There is a good view of the church from this footpath. Cross another stile beside a brick barn, and yet another stile takes you out to the road. Carry straight on and presently meet a road at right angles.

Turn left and keep left at the roundabout, along the road towards Waresley. At the next road junction go left along Little Gransden Lane. Go over a stream, and, where the road swings left in front of a cream-painted house hung with wall tiles, go right at the 'Public Footpath' sign onto a gravel drive between beech hedges. When you come to a white cottage on the left do not go through the gate but bear right along a narrow grassy path between hedges, which leads, very soon, to a stile.

You are now in a pasture with a fence and hedge on the right and some substantial trees. Gransden Wood is 100 yards away to the left. At the corner of this field follow the headland round to the left towards it. When you get close to the trees bear right, crossing a small rivulet, into the next field and follow the edge of the wood on your left. At this point you can see the spire of Waresley church ahead.

When you reach a grassy track coming from the road on the right and heading into the wood, you have a choice.

One option is to take the definitive right of way, which is straight ahead along a headland path just outside the wood. At the end of the field go left a yard and then follow beside the fence of the Water Treatment Plant until, at the far corner of the fence, you cross straight over a track which enters the wood over a wooden bridge.

The other option is to follow a route through the Waresley and Gransden Woods. Go left on the track into the wood, but immediately go right on a narrow path just inside the wood. In 100 yards the path turns left and widens. In a further 50 yards bear right on a narrower footpath. The path twists and turns but soon you leave the tall ash and sycamore trees and pass through a section of mixed coppiced woodland, mostly hazel and ash. Keep right where paths intersect, and descend to cross a wide timber bridge. Rising from the bridge, in 20 yards turn sharp right amid a taller stand of timber. Keep right until you pass an information board and cross a bridge at the edge of the wood. Here turn left.

To continue the walk, keep straight on along a grassy headland at the edge of Waresley Wood. Keep left round a corner of the wood. There is a large nestbox on a tree nearby, probably for an owl. When you reach another corner of the wood, at the end of two rows of trees, turn right on a grass avenue between the cupressus trees. Pass a lone oak and continue beside a ditch on the right. At the fence go left and out to a farm track in front of Wood Farm, which you passed at the beginning of the walk. Turn right and return to the Duncombe Arms and your starting point.

11 Houghton
The Three Horseshoes

Houghton lies between Huntingdon and St Ives, beside the river Great Ouse. As well as the village of Houghton, which is on the north bank, there are other pretty villages on the south bank, Hemingford Abbots and Hemingford Grey. Picturesque Houghton Mill was constructed in the 17th century, but there has been a water-mill on the site since the Domesday Book was compiled. St Ives, also on the Great Ouse, has a long history. The charter for its market, held on Mondays, was granted in 1290. It also has an annual fair every October on the Market Hill.

The Three Horseshoes, built in 1625, was once a coaching inn. It is a long, low building, forming most of one side of the Square. It faces the thatched Market Cross. The building has been extended many times. It has a large C-shaped lounge, around the central bar, with oak beams and inglenook fireplaces, and open fires in winter. A room is provided for family use, and children can play in the large garden. Overnight accommodation is available, too.

The menu includes chicken curry with rice, spaghetti bolognese, moussaka, chilli con carne, mushroom and fettuccine with salad, lasagne, goujons of plaice, and chicken and chips. Chocolate fudge cake and cream, ice-cream with raspberry sauce or apple and blackberry crispy

48

pancake rolls complete the meal. It is a friendly place, open all day (11 am to 11 pm) on Monday to Saturday, and the permitted hours on Sundays. While bar snacks are available at all times, more substantial meals are served from 12 noon to 2 pm and from 7 pm to 9.30 pm every day of the week. The real ales on offer are Greene King IPA, Ruddles Best Bitter, Marston's Pedigree Bitter and Courage Directors. For cider buffs there is Woodpecker and Scrumpy Jack. Well-behaved dogs are welcome.

Telephone: 01480 462410.

How to get there: Houghton is just south of the A1123, halfway between Huntingdon and St Ives. From Huntingdon, take the A141 Wisbech road and turn right at the edge of the town onto the A1123. Turn right in a mile to Houghton.

Parking: Cars can be parked in the Square, or beside the pub.

Length of the walk: 5½ miles. Map: OS Landranger sheet 153 Bedford, Huntingdon and surrounding area (inn GR 282722).

This walk follows watermeadows beside the river Great Ouse, passing the riverside villages of Hemingford Abbots and Hemingford Grey, to the town of St Ives.

The walk passes over the ancient stone bridge on the edge of St Ives, which was built around the 1400s by the Abbots of Ramsey. On the bridge is a chapel, dedicated to St Leger. The chapel is one of only three chapels on bridges in the country. At one time it was a house, and at another it was an inn. Now it is again a chapel, maintained by the County Council. The return is along a well used footpath on the north side of the Great Ouse river, beside woods called the Thicket and then on a country lane and across a campsite back to the start.

The Walk

From the Three Horseshoes go diagonally across the Square, passing the Market Cross, and go down narrow Church Lane. Near the end of the lane turn left and walk through the churchyard, keeping St Mary's church on the left. You come out to a road, turn right and walk to Houghton Mill at the end of the road. A narrow footpath leads through the mill building, and straight across a bridge over a weir. Pause here and look back at the mill.

Continue on a narrow tarmac path which leads to a footbridge beside Houghton Lock. Follow the path straight across Hemingford Meadow and cross the main arm of the river Great Ouse by a Bailey bridge to reach the end of a cul-de-sac.

Go down the road and turn left at the T-junction. This is the edge of Hemingford Abbots. Walk down the road, passing a number of

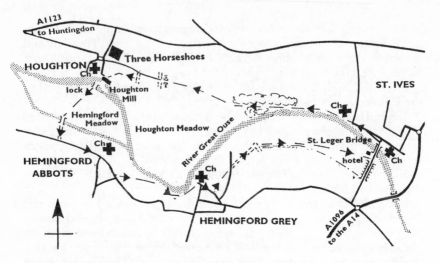

attractive thatched cottages. At the road junction keep straight on, along High Street, and soon pass the Axe and Compasses.

In about 200 yards and just after Beechers House on the left, and before Royal Oak Lane on the right, go left on a tarmac footpath which, in 100 yards, enters a meadow. Cross the field to a kissing-gate, which leads into a footpath between fences for about 100 yards and then to another gate. Walk the flood bank beside the river. On the left are some gnarled old trees. Soon reach a white kissing-gate and join an attractive riverside tarmac path.

The path joins the head of a cul-de-sac. Here keep left, close to the river, and follow a footpath sign along the tarmac path beside River Cottage. The river is very close, just beyond the cottage garden. When you reach St James's church, standing beside the river, turn right down the road from the church, passing more old thatched cottages. In just over 100 yards, and opposite No 22, turn left on to a gravel footpath, between fences. You come out to a road at a T-junction. Go straight forward along Meadow Lane. At the end, where a track goes right to a concrete drive into a farm, go straight ahead at the footpath sign and then through a kissing-gate into a large watermeadow.

Walk along the watermeadow, beside a fenced ditch on the right. After about ¼ mile, observe ahead the town of St Ives, with two churches, both having tall spires. The westernmost, the left-hand one, is the parish church of All Saints. When you get to the point where the parish church is directly to your left, and the ditch you are following swings round more sharply to the right, leave the edge of the meadow and walk towards the middle of a range of hotel buildings, half-left and lying somewhat to the right of the Free Church spire.

50

As you approach the hotel complex there is a gate with a stile beside it. Go over the stile and cross the car park to the road. Turn left and go across the ancient stone St Leger Bridge over the river Great Ouse, passing the chapel on your right.

From the bridge, continue along Bridge Street for 100 yards and at the T-junction turn left into Crown Street.

Enter The Broadway. Pass on the left the Norris Museum and then a long tapering green fronting the river. On the right is the Methodist church, built of brown carstone. When the road goes right you go straight ahead, along a snicket, to the churchyard of All Saints parish church. At this church since the 1600s, once a year, schoolchildren have diced to win bibles.

Leave the churchyard on the far side by a gate, go a few yards left and continue beside the river on the Ouse Valley Way, a good tarmac path with lighting and occasional seats. A road comes in from the right but keep straight on. Go through a squeezer stile and then you are in a wooded area, with, on your right, what is known as The Thicket. Keep on the tarmac path, passing on the left, a gate into Houghton Meadow, a nature reserve. Eventually, go over a small stream and, immediately after, cross a bridleway going left and right.

Keep straight on along the tarmac road. Turn left immediately before the first house on the left and in 50 yards, at a waymark, turn right at the corner of the rear garden of that house, along a narrow cinder track. In 200 yards go left over a stile and cross the campsite on the route indicated by the waymarks. Go out of the campsite by a stile, a few feet to the left of the vehicular exit, to Houghton Mill.

Turn right, away from the river, and walk along the road to the Square, Potto Brown's statue and the Three Horseshoes.

Other local attractions: Houghton Mill is owned by the National Trust. It is open from 2 pm to 5.30 pm at weekends and on bank holiday Mondays from the end of March to the end of June, and from the beginning of September till mid October. In July and August it is open from Saturday through to Wednesday. The mill machinery has been restored and milling takes place on Sundays from 2.30 pm to 5 pm. You can buy the wholemeal flour. For exact details phone the custodian on 01480 301494.

The Norris Museum, in a picturesque riverside setting in St Ives, not far from the old stone bridge, is well worth a visit. Opening times are Monday to Friday 10 am to 1 pm and 2 pm to 5 pm, Saturday 10 am to 12 noon and 2 pm to 5 pm, and Sunday 2 pm to 5 pm, from May to September, and during October to April from 10 am to 1 pm and 2 pm to 4 pm Monday to Friday, and on Saturday from 10 am to 12 noon. Telephone: 01480 465101.

⑫ Ramsey
The Angel

The country surrounding the isolated town of Ramsey is dotted with numerous small woods and the walk is pleasantly rural. Ramsey is a small town almost surrounded by the flat fenland of north Cambridgeshire. The church and the abbey stand at the eastern end of a narrow main street. By contrast, the other main street of Ramsey is surprisingly wide with part of a central strip given over to car parking. Originally there were roads on both sides of a waterway called High Lode which led to the old river Nene. Houses overlooking the waterway fronted both the roads. The waterway was eventually covered over, making this wide road.

At the northern end of the town, just beyond a large brick warehouse, there is a quay where narrow boats and other craft, which ply the waterways of Cambridgeshire and come to Ramsey along the High Lode, can moor. Close to the quay you can see the end of the culvert which runs below the road.

Just after setting out for the walk you will reach the church of St Thomas à Becket, which stands at the end of the main street. It is surrounded on both sides by a grassy open space. To the north is Church Green, with a delightful group of buildings on its far side, while to the south are the remains of the gatehouse of the Benedictine Abbey, which was founded in AD 969. The gatehouse, which can be visited, dates from 1475. It is but a shadow of the original gatehouse, which must have been quite grand. Adjacent, stands the entrance to the grounds of the Abbey School, Ramsey. It was designed by Sir John Soane who remodelled Wimpole Hall, near Cambridge. After the dissolution of the monasteries during Henry VIII's reign, much of the abbey stone was plundered and was used for building some of Cambridge's colleges.

The Angel is a popular pub and a welcoming one. The lounge bar – the dining area – is comfortably furnished, with plentiful upholstered seating around the walls and elsewhere beside small tables. The other bar has billiards and darts. Outside in the spacious yard is a large covered area, set with benches and tables. In July and August this is festooned with the delicate white, hanging flowers and greenery of the silver lace vine, a plant which grows at a prodigious rate.

The food is good and served speedily. Home-made dishes include steak and kidney pie, lasagne and chicken curry. Vegetarian meals, such as curry, lasagne, cashew nut balls and mushrooms with cream and garlic sauce, are also on offer. Many, however, will be tempted by the large all-meat mixed grill – pork, lamb and beef steaks and Cumberland sausage with chips, peas, mushroom and onion rings, or by a 16 oz rump steak. Gammon steak, half a roast chicken and fish dishes are on the menu, too. A variety of sweets is available. Webster's Yorkshire Bitter and Courage Directors real ales are served, and Scrumpy Jack cider. Children have their own menu, and they can let off steam in the covered area and yard at the rear. Dogs, other than guide dogs, are not permitted in the pub.

The opening times are from 10 am to 11 pm six days a week, with the usual Sunday hours. On weekdays and Saturdays, meals are served from 10 am to 2 pm and from 6 pm to 9.30 pm. Sunday times are 12 noon to 2 pm and 7 pm to 9.30 pm.

Telephone: 01487 813226.

How to get there: Ramsey lies about 10 miles north of Huntingdon and can be reached from the A141 Chatteris to Huntingdon road. Follow the B1040 through Warboys to Ramsey. The Angel is on the left, close to the T-junction in the centre of the town.

Parking: The large pub car park is reached via Great Whyte and then Little Whyte, which is parallel to High Street and behind the pub. There is some street parking along the main street, and a car parking area in Great Whyte, just round the corner.

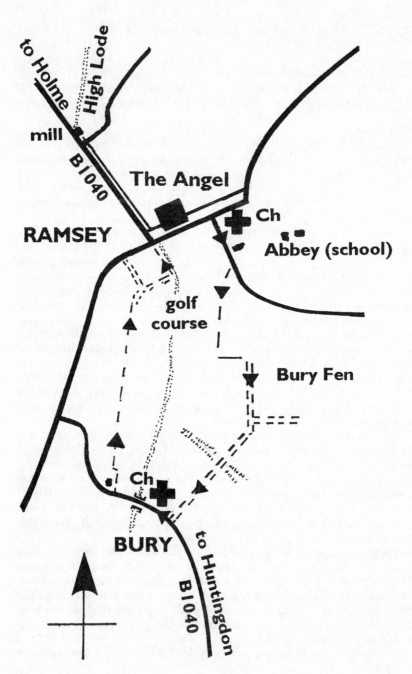

to Holme

High Lode

mill

B1040

The Angel

Ch

RAMSEY

Abbey (school)

golf course

Bury Fen

Ch

BURY

to Huntingdon

B1040

54

Length of the walk: 2 miles. Map: OS Landranger sheet 142 Peterborough (inn GR 288851).

This short and easy walk, after passing the church and the remains of the ancient gatehouse of the former Benedictine Abbey, goes south across the golf course and Bury Fen to the village of Bury. The return skirts the golf course along field paths.

The Walk

From the Angel go left along High Street. Go to the church at the end and have a look at the green, surrounded by attractive yellowy-brick buildings, just north of the church. The church of St Thomas à Becket, with Church Green and Ramsey Abbey Gatehouse, now in the hands of the National Trust, make a delightful group of buildings amid a tranquil, grassy setting.

Having looked at the church and the green, retrace your steps a little and go left in front of the gatehouse and an entrance to the school, and turn left into Hollow Lane, the road to the Ramsey Hollow sports centre. In 200 yards turn right off the lane, through a kissing-gate beside a white farm gate, onto the public footpath across the golf course. There is a warning to beware of golf balls. Turn half-left and keep strictly to the path marked by blue waymarked posts.

At the far side of the golf course take a narrow path through the hedge and climb onto a bank. Go left on a lane between hedges. In 100 yards the track turns sharp right and now you are on a lovely, 5 yard wide, grassy bank which is ½ yard higher than the fields on either side. It follows a deep ditch on the left. Bury church, a midway point of the walk, can be seen half-right, whilst over to the left is a broad sweep of fenland stretching towards Chatteris.

Pass, on the left, a track from a collection of barns ½ mile away, and keep straight on, then follow the track half right. Cross the route of the former railway. You can see it stretching away on an embankment to the left, and to the right skirting the golf course. Join a tarmac road, Meadow Lane, and walk down it to the main road, the B1040, and turn right. This is the village of Bury. Shortly, at Holy Cross church, go through the churchyard, pass the south porch and return to the road.

From here you see ahead a little valley, through which the golf course is laid out. Go down the road and over the bridge. Keep on the road for 200 yards and go right over a stile by a footpath sign, immediately before the Old School House, a single storey stone-built dwelling. The golf course is on the right. Some 50 yards from the road go left over a stile and then follow a path just outside the golf course fence. Cross a stile and a wooden bridge. Ignore a path off to the left, and keep in the same direction as before, with a hedge on the right. Cross a narrow ditch by a plank and go straight on along a headland path beside a field on the left.

About 30 yards from the corner of the field turn right over a timber bridge across a ditch, onto a narrow footpath. On the right there is a deep ditch, with the golf course beyond and a bank on the left. When you reach a junction of paths, turn right on to a well-used broad path between hedges, with a deep ditch on the left. The path leads to the bank of a wide river.

Turn left at first beside the river and then go past single storey motel buildings, through an arch and out to the road. Turn right to reach the Angel in 50 yards.

The wide river that you followed for a few yards before reaching the motel, flows in a culvert under the town, beneath Great Whyte and the car park beside it, northwards for ¼ mile, to emerge at the mill, into a navigable waterway called High Lode.

Other local attractions: On the edge of the town is Ramsey Rural Museum (reached by a lane opposite the town's cemetery). It is open from 2 pm to 5 pm on Thursdays and Sundays from April till September, and at other times by appointment. Telephone: 01487 815715. There is a display of agricultural implements, a schoolroom set out in the style of late Victorian times, various rooms furnished with period furniture, old toys and recreational items, and a shop as it would have been in years long gone. The trades display room houses a fascinating collection of the tools used by various skilled tradesmen.

At the northern end of Ramsey is a small dock on High Lode, with a little public parking where you may watch what is going on. A modern-style windmill is in the background.

Ramsey Abbey Gatehouse, now in the hands of the National Trust, is open to the public from the beginning of April until the end of October, daily from 10 am to 5 pm.

Holme Fen Posts can be combined with a visit to Ramsey, which is only 5 miles from Holme Fen. Go north-west along the B1040. In 3 miles turn right and cross the river Nene. Then in ¼ mile go left on the B660 to Holme. Cross the railway and turn right. Take the next turning right, recross the railway and continue for ½ mile. The posts are on the right, just off the road, beyond a drainage ditch and reached by crossing a narrow footbridge (GR 203894).

13 Litlington
The Crown

At the south-west corner of Cambridgeshire, close to the Hertfordshire border, lie the twin villages of Steeple Morden and Guilden Morden, with Litlington close by. This area is arable farmland with shallow valleys draining northwards to the river Cam. To the south of the villages is a flat plain which meets the foot of a chalk escarpment about 2 miles away. Midway between Litlington and Steeple Morden are the remains of a Second World War airbase. Alongside the road, a memorial commemorates the exploits of over 2,000 United States airmen who served here with the 355th Fighter Group between July 1943 and July 1945. They flew Mustang and Thunderbolt aircraft and damaged or destroyed over 1,500 enemy aircraft.

The Crown, built in 1790 as a pub and a smithy, stands on a corner opposite the village post office. Tables and benches are set out on the broad forecourt in front. At the rear of the building is a petanque piste, and the pub team plays regularly in a local league. Inside, a large collection of aviation photographs and memorabilia connected with the former airbase is displayed around the walls.

The broad range of items on the menu includes rump steak au poivre, Cajun-style butterfly chicken breasts which are cooked using paprika, white pepper and cayenne, a rack of barbecue-style pork spare ribs, breaded plaice filled with prawns and mushrooms, lasagne verdi and cottage pie. Irish stew, chilli con carne and mushroom fettuccine are also served. Indian food is served on Thursday evenings and Greek food on Friday evenings. Besides all that there is the Crown Grill Bar and the Crown Burger Bar, one of whose dishes is significantly called 'The Belt Buster'. The sweet menu offers a choice of hot chocolate fudge cake, apple and blackberry pancake, apple and sultana sponge or toffee apple and pecan pie. Greene King IPA and Abbot and Rayments Special Bitter are the real ales. Red Rock draught cider is also on offer. Meals are served at lunchtimes and in the evenings, but not on Monday evenings or on Sundays. Children dining with their parents are welcome and dogs are allowed on the premises, if well-behaved.

Telephone: 01763 852439.

How to get there: Litlington lies north of the A505 (Royston bypass to Baldock road) and is 3 miles from Royston.

Parking: The car park is at the rear of the Crown. You may find some on-street parking in the village one-way system.

Length of the walk: 4½ miles. Map: OS Landranger sheet 153 Bedford, Huntingdon and surrounding area (inn GR 311427).

From the centre of Litlington, the walk passes the church and then takes cross-field paths to Steeple Morden. It then follows, southwards, the shallow valley of Cheney Water, a tiny stream which flows to the river Rhee and thence to the river Cam. After crossing part of the former airfield the walk joins Ashwell Street, a 7 mile long cart track running eastwards from the village of Ashwell, to return to the start. Ashwell Street is part of the Icknield Way long distance path which runs from Ivinghoe Beacon to Knettishall Heath.

The Walk
Leaving the Crown, turn right and go along the road towards the church. Pass the old school, which is now a garage, on the left and take the tarmac path through the churchyard. Pass the south porch and leave the churchyard in the opposite corner by a steel kissing-gate in the shade of an old yew tree.

Go left for 10 yards and cross the road. Keep the tiny sub-station on your right and take the path across the field, signed 'Public Footpath to Steeple Morden 1½'. The path is roughly parallel to the field boundary on the right. At the far side of the field cross a ditch by a sleeper bridge and go straight on in the same direction as before, across the next field, to a gap between two trees in the opposite hedge. Keep in the same

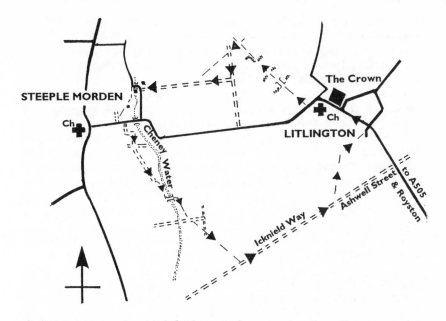

direction, across the third field, towards a couple of small trees on the far side, where you stride a shallow ditch beside a coppiced ash tree on the left. Go left for a few yards to the corner of the field, then turn right, following the field boundary on the left. In a few yards, where the field boundary swings to the left, go forward in the same general direction as before but bearing slightly to the left.

About halfway across this field meet another footpath at right angles – don't get confused with the tram lines, which are tracks made by crop spraying machinery, it is a path which comes from the right-hand far corner of the field. Turn left on it, going roughly south-west. At the field boundary there is a waymark. Reach a grassy cart track going left and right.

Turn left along the track for about 250 yards and turn right at a T-junction of tracks, at a sign saying 'No Horses Footpath Only'. Half-right whilst walking along this farm track you can see, in the distance, the spire-topped tower of Guilden Morden church. In ½ mile, at the end of the cart track, you come to a road. Go right and almost immediately swing round left along the road, and cross a small stream called Cheney Water. Note the steel railings here. Where the road bends right again, go left at a 'Footpath' sign on a concrete track, and then, at a waymark, bear to the right along a narrow footpath, following the fence on the left.

Cross a stile at the corner of the field, into a pasture. Bear slightly right, keeping the corners of the field and the buildings close on your left. At the second fence corner go slightly right to the far right-hand corner of the field. Exit over a stile and turn left to the village street of Steeple Morden, opposite Cheney Close. Go left for 50 yards and turn right, at a footpath sign, along Black Lane.

The lane, which is just a footpath, turns left and then right where a footpath joins it and in a few yards joins the end of a tarmac road. Soon reach a road off to the left and a telephone box. Here go straight on, along a tarmac road, signed 'Public Footpath to Ashwell Street', past some cottages.

At the end of the houses the road reverts to a grassy cart track which, in 300 yards, ends at a crop division. From this point go half-left towards the trees, 50 yards away, enter the tree belt on a narrow footpath and continue through the trees. In amongst the woodland to the left is the tiny Cheney Water.

Where the path divides, keep to the right on the higher ground for a few yards. When you see a bridge on the left, go down towards the stream again and over the substantial footbridge. Climb for a short distance out of the valley and go over a stile without a footpiece, into a field, and turn right alongside the fence on the right. There is a large farmhouse beyond the fence.

Where the fence on the right ends you come to a cart track at right angles. Here, go slightly left of the direction you have been on before, across a field. Obliquely cross a tarmac road, probably a former airfield taxiway, and later cross a cart track, but still keep straight on. At the far side of the field you come to a lane with hedges on both sides. This is part of the Icknield Way. Note that electricity wires on wooden poles follow the line of this path. Turn left towards Litlington.

In about ¼ mile you follow a short piece of concrete road, doubtless vestigial remains of the airfield. Where the concrete ends, continue along a grass track. Pass on the left a concrete road, going at right angles, and then at a waymark turn half-left, leaving the 'Icknield Way Riders Route'. You are now on a grassy footpath, with wheel marks, which swings gradually round to the right and you come to the end of a small gravel road, pass some farm buildings, then some cottages and turn left into Church Street. Keep straight on to reach, on the right, your start at the Crown in Litlington.

14 Bourn
The Golden Lion

The village of Bourn, 9 miles west of Cambridge city, lies less than a mile east of the A1198, which was the Roman road, Ermine Street, from London to Lincoln and on to York, running straight as a die for mile after mile. The narrow road opposite the Golden Lion leads to the church and to Bourn Hall. The church of St Helena and St Mary has a lead covered, wooden spire that over the years has twisted and inclined to one side. Below the bell tower, by the font, is a floor maze in red and black tiles. Such a maze in a parish church is a rarity in English churches. The tenor bell, one of eight bells, is inscribed 'I to the church the living call, and to the grave do summon all'. Standing at the end of the drive, among 22 acres of parkland, is red-brick Bourn Hall. A Jacobean country house, with Elizabethan origins, it has been much enlarged. It was a family home until 1980, when it became Bourn Hall Clinic, an infertility clinic of international repute.

The Golden Lion, a friendly pub, which also offers overnight accommodation, is well over 200 years old. The public rooms occupy the whole of the front of the building, with the two bars vaguely separated by an open screen. The walls are decorated with photographs of the family's show jumping triumphs and by many of their trophies.

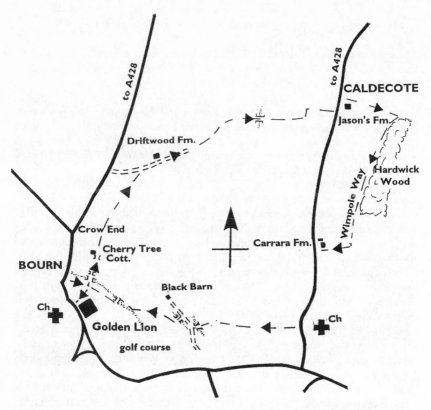

If you parked in the yard you may have seen some of their mounts. Children are well catered for in a garden area with play apparatus.

On the menu are such dishes as ocean pie, cod, plaice or scampi and chips, gammon and pineapple, lamb Madras, mixed grill, chicken tikka masala, lamb rogan josh and hot spicy chicken. So, too, are apple pie, cheesecake, banana split and chocolate gâteau. Meals are available from 12 noon to 2 pm and from 6 pm to 8.30 pm, but are not served on Sunday evenings. The real ales on sale are Boddingtons and Flowers IPA, and Strongbow draught cider is on offer, too. Dogs are welcome if well-behaved.

Telephone: 01954 719305.

How to get there: Go to Caxton Gibbet roundabout at the junction between the A428 Cambridge to St Neots road and the A1198 Huntingdon to Royston road. Go south on the A1198 and in just under 2 miles turn left to Bourn. In a mile turn right at a T-junction. The Golden Lion is in the centre of the village, on the left.

Parking: There is plenty of parking in the yard behind the pub.

Length of the walk: 5½ miles. Map: OS Landranger sheets 153 Bedford, Huntingdon and surrounding area and 154 Cambridge and Newmarket, with most of the walk on the latter (inn GR 325564).

From Bourn, the walk goes north-east, along a well defined, and probably ancient, cart track, to the village of Caldecote. Rising slightly beyond the village, the route joins the Wimpole Way, a long distance track leading towards Wimpole Hall, going beside woods to Caldecote church. The return is along field paths to skirt the Bourn golf course, and back to the start.

The Walk
From the Golden Lion go right along the road, bearing right past the war memorial and passing several excellent half-timbered houses. Keep right down Alms Hill and, opposite Kingfisher Close, turn right at a footpath sign reading 'Public Footpath Crow End ¼ Caldecote 1½'. Cross a stile and go over a meadow on a well-used grass path. When you reach the gravel drive, underneath some electricity cables, turn left on another well-trodden grass path and cross a concrete bridge over the Bourn Brook.

Cross a single sleeper bridge and go over a stile into a grass field, then follow the hedge on the right. Pass to the right of the thatched, white Cherry Tree Cottage where you cross two stiles about 5 yards apart, and then a timber bridge. The path leads into a pleasant little lane which passes several isolated thatched, white cottages which are very picturesque. At the junction where a track goes left, go straight on. The track becomes a narrow hollow lane, that is an old way which, over the passage of time, has become lower than the surrounding fields. Pass one or two buildings on the left, including a white farmhouse with a slate roof. Leave the hollow lane and climb out to a concrete farm road at right angles.

Go right along the concrete farm road for nearly ½ mile, passing a chalet bungalow, Driftwood Farm, and then Driftwood Stables, to the end of the concrete road, at the entrance to a water treatment plant. Continue in the same direction, now on a cart track. In about ¼ mile the track crosses a stream and then enters a wide green lane between hedges. The lane ends at a field. Here make a right turn and continue on a headland bridleway, with a hedge on the right. Come out to the road at Caldecote and turn left. Just after the tall cupressus on the right and in front of Jason's Farm, go right, on the bridleway towards Hardwick. At first it is a grassy track between hedges, later the hedge on the left gives way to a ranch-style fence.

When you reach the edge of the wood there is a T-junction of tracks.

63

Here turn right beside Hardwick Wood, along the Wimpole Way. Note the waymark's distinctive symbol. Shortly, snake slightly left to cross a cartbridge over a ditch and go straight on, between bluebell woods on the left and a ditch on the right. About 250 yards after the wood ends, swing round to the right by the waymark, ignoring a footpath off to the left, and in about 300 yards turn left along a road.

When you reach Caldecote church on the left, go right at a sign 'Public Footpath to Bourn 1½'. Continue up a small ramp, a drive to a house, then keep alongside the hedge on the left. In the corner of the orchard go over a stile and straight across the field to a gate. Continue on a grassy cart track, with a ditch on your right. You come to a waymark at the end of the field and look down into a shallow valley.

Here descend a low bank and go half-left towards a cart-bridge you can see in the valley bottom. Cross the bridge and go towards a black barn. Halfway to the barn, at a waymark, turn left over another cartbridge. Cross to the edge of the golf course and turn right. Continue, at first with a hedge and then later a deep stream, the Bourn Brook, on the left.

Go left over a concrete bridge and turn right. When you get underneath the electricity wires, turn left on a well-walked path looking towards the church. Cross a stile and walk on, with a hedge on the right. Go over another stile into a narrow way between a fence on the left and a brick wall on the right, and out by a stile to the road beside the Golden Lion.

Other local attractions: The black, weather-boarded post mill, Bourn Windmill, is at a high point on the north-west edge of Bourn, out on the Caxton road. The mill, which is documented from the early 1600s is the oldest one in the county. Just 30 yards west of Mill Cottage is a gap in the hedge leading into a minuscule car park. A path leads from here, round two sides of a paddock, to the mill, which you may wander round and under, but not in. As you stand beneath the mill and see how it is mounted on massive wooden trestles and cross-trees, which in turn are supported on four brick stanchions, its latent power is most impressive.

Arrington
The Hardwicke Arms

15

The district is one of undulating rich farmland, well dotted with small woods and plenty of mature trees. Just to the north of the inn is the 350 acre estate of Wimpole Hall and its associated Wimpole Home Farm, owned by the National Trust. The Earls of Hardwicke were the owners of Wimpole Hall in the 18th and 19th centuries. The road past the Hardwicke Arms, now called Ermine Way, was the ancient Roman road, Ermine Street, from London to the North. The grand entrance gates to Wimpole Hall which face onto the old road are seldom used now.

The elegant Hardwicke Arms is a 13th century coaching inn. It is a long hotel, stretched along the road frontage in the main street of Arrington. Inside, the atmosphere is friendly and welcoming. On each of the tables is a small vase of fresh flowers. All manner of beer jugs are displayed in the main bar which, with the lounge bar and snug, is perfect for a lunchtime or evening meal. The comfortable, more formal, restaurant is oak-panelled. A no-smoking area is provided. Overnight accommodation is also available if you wish to stay in the area.

The changing menu is always interesting. Fried Camembert with port and cranberry sauce, and salmon and scallops in filo pastry are not dishes that one sees often on inn menus. Other meals served are pork curry, country stewpot, chicken chasseur with red wine and goujons of plaice with chips, peas and tartare sauce. An assortment of gâteaux, white chocolate fudge cake and 'blond bombshell' make a sweet course irresistible. On Sundays there is a lunchtime carvery. Vegetarian dishes, such as Stroganov with wild and basmati rice, and fettuccine with onions, mushrooms and tomatoes, are also available. Children have their own menu, and a garden area in which to play. Meals are served at lunchtime and in the evenings seven days a week, except that food is not available on Sunday evenings in the winter. The real ales are Greene King IPA, Bass, Adnams and a guest beer. Dry Blackthorn draught cider is also on offer. Dogs are not permitted in the inn, except, of course, guide dogs.

Telephone: 01223 208802

How to get there: Arrington lies on the A1198 road between Huntingdon and Royston. From the north, leave the A14 at the Godmanchester interchange then follow the A1198 for 13 miles. From Cambridge and the east take the A428 towards St Neots. Turn left onto the A1198 at the Caxton Gibbet roundabout. The Hardwicke Arms is on the main road in the village.

Parking: The inn has ample parking at the rear, and it is also possible to park on the roadside.

Length of the walk: 5½ miles. Map: OS Landranger sheets 154 Cambridge and Newmarket and 153 Bedford, Huntingdon and surrounding area (inn GR 328502).

The walk starts along the drive, through the broad parkland, to pass the front of Wimpole Hall. Later the path climbs past farms comprising part of the estate. Here each field you pass has an information board describing the present crop, saying what was planted in the previous season and what is planned for the next crop. The notice also explains what treatment(s) the field has received. At the top of the hill – halfway round the walk – pass reservoirs and an Ordnance Survey trig pillar. Not surprisingly, from this high point there are wide views of the surrounding countryside. The return is along rural footpaths and bridleways to Arrington.

The Walk
From the Hardwicke Arms walk north along the road, Ermine Way, towards Huntingdon. In about 150 yards, by the massive wrought-iron ornamental entrance gates of Wimpole Hall, go through an iron wicket gate to the right of the main gates, and walk along the tarmac drive. Pass through an iron kissing-gate beside a cattle grid.

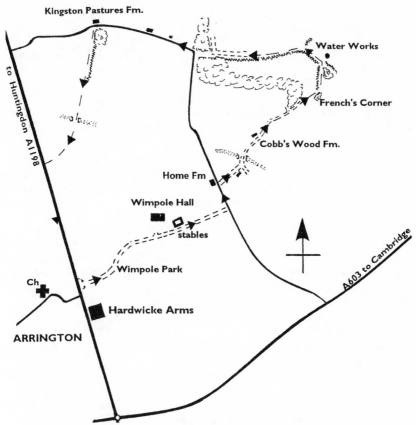

Follow the tarmac drive, passing through two more kissing-gates, as it sweeps round to the left and then to the right, crossing parallel to the front of Wimpole Hall, 100 yards away to the left, then pass the red-brick stable block on your left. Continue on the drive for ¼ mile to reach a road. Turn left along it. Pass a telephone box and opposite the black weather-boarded thatched barns of Home Farm turn right along a wide gravel farm track. Before setting off along this track read the informative board at the junction. You will be following the walk described on the board for some of the way.

Pass on the right a bungalow, Keeper's Cottage, then keep left, crossing a bridge, over a small but deep stream. Later pass a cream-washed farmhouse, Cobb's Wood Farm. The surfaced road ends here. Continue straight on along an earth farm track, with a ditch on your right. In 100 yards or so the ditch on the right ends and you bear slightly right, up the hill towards the woods.

When almost at the top of the hill, where you pass a wood on the

67

left, pause on the seat to enjoy the panoramic views. Where the wood ends you carry straight on, still on a cart track, with a hedge and ditch on the left. When the cart track turns right, keep straight on, on a wide grass path, with a small triangle of young mixed woodland on the right. This is called French's Corner.

In about 50 yards, at the far end of the wood on the right, turn left at the waymark with 'Ramblers' written in poker work on the shaft. You are still on a grassy headland path with a wide field on the right. You now come to the corner of the field, where there is a damaged steel footpath sign. Go left towards the water tanks of the Cambridge Water Company, and there bear left between the water company's fence on the right and the hedge on the left. The path narrows a little bit, later widening out into a delightful grassy bridleway. Note the Ordnance Survey trig point. From here you can see wide views.

As you approach some woodland the path becomes a cart track. After following the edge of the wood for about 100 yards the cart track goes right. You go straight on along a bridleway through the wood. You come out to a road where it makes a sharp bend. Go straight on along the rural road, passing a farm on your right. Do not turn off right when 'The Wimpole Way' goes right, but keep on the road until you reach Kingston Pastures Farm, a three-storey building on the right. Here, opposite a barn, go left at a footpath sign, on a grassy headland, with a hedge on the left. When the hedge and its few trees end you then have a deep ditch on your left.

At the end of the field you go through a hedge, and are confronted by a wide field, where the route has been marked out. Should the markers not be there you would navigate by going initially towards a prominent house on the skyline, and then later swing left a little to the far side of the field to cross a stile and then walk across the pasture down to a bridge, and a double farm gate. Keep on in the same direction to go through another gate. Follow a grass path along (possibly) a crop division, still going in the same basic direction. The well-used path curves right, leading to a sleeper bridge and out to the road. Turn left. There is a footway on the far side of the road. Follow this all the way down into Arrington.

Other local attractions: The National Trust property Wimpole Hall, a large 18th century style mansion, is a few hundred yards away. There is also the NT farm, Wimpole Home Farm – a working farm with rare breeds, and with a collection of farm machinery as used here over the last 200 years. Both are open from the end of March until the beginning of November, but not on Mondays or Fridays, except bank holiday Mondays. They are also open on Fridays from mid July to mid August. For times ring 01223 207257.

16 Earith
The Crown

The river Great Ouse dominates the area. At Earith it makes an almost right-angle turn to wander across the fens to Ely before turning north towards the sea at the Wash. It was from Earith that the engineer Vermuyden in 1630 cut a straight drainage channel to take the Ouse floodwater directly to Denver where it rejoined the Great Ouse, thus bypassing the wide loop of the river through Ely. Somewhat surprisingly, Vermuyden, 20 years later, returned to cut another, wider drainage channel parallel to the earlier channel and about ¼ mile apart. These channels are named respectively the Old and the New Bedford river, after the 4th Earl of Bedford who financed the project. However, the channels are currently named, less romantically, the Eighty Foot Drain and the Hundred Foot Drain.

The Crown is on the main road through the village of Earith, and at the rear runs the river Great Ouse. There is a garden alongside the river, on the pub's own river frontage, with a floating landing stage for boat mooring. There are two separate bars, plus a restaurant. You could say that one bar is for the younger folk, with pool, darts and suchlike, while the other is for the staider customer who wishes to sit

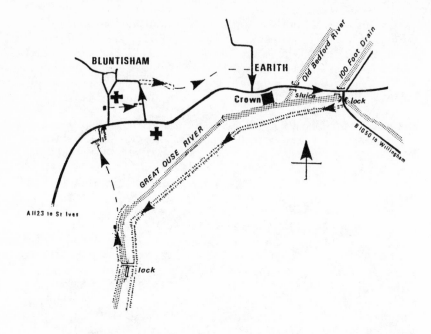

on upholstered chairs or stools and eat or drink at small tables, with beaten-copper tops, in a cosy atmosphere. The restaurant leading off the more sedate bar is well-appointed. In the lounge bar are collections of pottery dogs and model cars, larger than Dinky toys, in showcases. China plates depicting different aircraft decorate the walls. At times there is live music.

The menu is wide. Choose from Cajun chicken, gammon steak, home-made steak and kidney pie, mixed grill, steak with whisky sauce, chicken breast in a port wine sauce, seafood platter, salmon steak in a hollandaise sauce, spinach and ricotta cheese cannelloni and much more, followed by toffee apple and pecan pie, profiteroles, treacle pudding and custard, spotted dick and custard and chocolate pudding with chocolate sauce, or Crown meringue. Children dining with their parents are welcome. A good play area is provided by the river, but of course close supervision will be necessary down there. Such real ales as John Smith's, Marston's Pedigree Bitter and a guest ale are served, along with Dry Blackthorn cider and sweet Autumn Gold. The pub is closed at Monday lunchtimes and no food is served on a Monday. Otherwise the usual hours apply. Dogs may only go in the public bar and in the garden.

Telephone: 01487 841442.

How to get there: From the north, go to Huntingdon and then follow the A1123 to St Ives. Continue on the A1123 (Ely road) and in 5 miles reach Earith. From the south, go north from Cambridge towards Huntingdon on the A14. At the grade-separated interchange take the B1050. Go through Longstanton and Willingham and 2 miles further on turn left at a T–junction. The Crown is in the main street.

Parking: The Crown has a good car park at the rear. The main road is too narrow for parking, but alternatively there is a car park behind the village hall to the west of the Crown. This also has access to the river.

Length of the walk: 5½ miles. Map: OS Landranger sheet 142 Peterborough. This shows 90% of the walk – the other 10% is on sheet 154 Cambridge and Newmarket, but that map is by no means necessary (inn GR 386748).

From the Crown, the walk passes the sluices and lock where the Old and New Bedford rivers join the river Great Ouse. The walk continues south-westward on a flood protection wall beside the Great Ouse, which is crossed at a lock near the village of Over. The return is along part of the Ouse Valley Way, through Bluntisham and then alongside an orchard back to Earith.

The Walk

From the Crown turn right along the main street, the A1123, and at the end of the village cross a bridge over the Old Bedford river. Look to the right to see the great sluice gates which control the level of water. Then in ¼ mile cross the next bridge, over the New Bedford river or the Hundred Foot Drain, which is another of the drainage canals built by Vermuyden. Vessels are warned that navigating this canal may be dangerous.

After crossing the Hundred Foot Drain turn right along the road signed 'Willingham'. In just under 100 yards cross a bridge over a lock which enables craft to continue along the river Great Ouse. Immediately after the lock, turn right along a tarmac track, passing, on the left, Lock House, and cross a stile onto the river's flood protection bank. This is the Ouse Valley Way.

The flood protection bank is at least 15 ft above the field, which appears to be at an even lower level than the water in the river on the right. Away to the south are the very flat fields of this area. You can see church towers and spires a long way off. On the right flows the river Great Ouse and, beyond, the backs of the houses in Earith.

At a fence cross a stile beside a gate. You can see half-right the spire on the church of Bluntisham-cum-Earith. At another stile beside a gate, cross the former railway line – you can see the remains of the bridge piers on the right. Keep on the flood bank, crossing a number of stiles. Just over a mile from the old railway, and immediately before an isolated house on the left, you come to a bridge across the low-lying land beside the river. Go across this bridge, which leads to a lock and two huge sluice gates across the Great Ouse. Then follow another concrete bridge across low-lying land to reach the river wall on the opposite side. Turn right along the river wall. You will now see the church spire directly ahead. When you come to a small brick pumping station on the left, cross a stile which says 'Ouse Valley Way' and in about 100 yards bear left, leaving the river and the Ouse Valley Way.

You are on a grass headland path, which later becomes a grass path between crops. Cross a culvert, keeping straight on along a cart track. At the corner of the field follow the cart track round to the right and then in about 100 yards go left along the lane to a road. This is the edge of Bluntisham. Turn right on the road and in 50 yards turn left along Bluntisham High Street, the road to Colne and Somersham.

Opposite the former day school, a single storey building on the left, go right on a tarmac path. A brick building on the left, surrounded by a churchyard, is the old Bluntisham Baptist Meeting House, built in 1787 and rebuilt 87 years later. Keep straight on along this tarmac path, past some houses on the left. Join St Mary's Close and in 30 yards turn left along a road. Where the road you are following swings left, turn right along a tarmac lane with a 'No Through Road' sign. Pass the playing field on the left and at the end of it the tarmac road becomes a wide lane with an orchard on the right, ending at a gate into another orchard.

Go through the gate. Do not bear right along a well-trodden path with a hedge on the right, but go slightly left on a less well-used path, almost straight on from where you were before, to cross the end of an orchard. The path will lead to a wide grass path along the line of some overhead electricity cables. There is a ditch on the right. You can see the river ¼ mile away, to the right. You will come to an orchard on the left and a large industrial storage shed on the right. At the far side of the orchard cross a stile and then continue in the same direction across a pasture and leave by a kissing-gate into a short lane, called Whybrow's Lane, and out to a road. Turn right. At the T–junction turn left onto the A1123 towards Stretham, to return to the Crown.

Other local attractions: The Ouse Valley Way is a 26 mile walk through the former Huntingdonshire, following the attractive river valley of the Great Ouse. For most of its length the path is along the river edge. The route gives an excellent opportunity to experience the land of Oliver Cromwell – a countryside of rolling landscapes, river valleys and watermeadows. It passes bustling market towns and picturesque villages. There are seven leaflets describing the walk.

17 Grantchester
The Rupert Brooke

Grantchester, not far to the south-west of Cambridge, has a quiet charm. The Cam, the distant views of Cambridge's dreaming spires with the unforgettable roof of King's College Chapel and the watermeadows combine to make this walk a peaceful, enjoyable one. The village is closely associated with the poet Rupert Brooke, who, after graduating from King's College, lived here, some of the time at the Old Vicarage. On the war memorial in the churchyard you can find his name, though he is buried on the Greek island of Skyros where he died in 1915 at the age of 27.

Changes in level in this pleasant pub make the subdivisions of the interior more subtle, and help create a homely atmosphere, to which the friendly staff contribute. It will surprise few people that the time on the clock in the Rupert Brooke is permanently set at ten to three. Some of the poet's writings are displayed on the walls. Old farm implements – flails, drainage tools and gins – are also used as decoration, while on a high shelf are many glass and stone bottles and a variety of kitchen mincing and slicing machines. For the comfort of the really lazy who find turning round on traditional bar stools wearisome, two which swivel and have backs are provided.

The menu is broad and offers plenty of healthy choices, with steak and kidney pie, Tandoori chicken on rice, sweet and sour vegetables, lamb cutlets, chicken Kiev, nut cutlets with tomato and herb sauce, sirloin steak, peppercorn steak, gammon steak, chicken provençale, pie of the day, salmon steak and much more. A variety of sweets is displayed in a cabinet, and spotted dick and cheese and biscuits are on offer as well. The real ales are Brakspear, Flowers IPA, Boddingtons, 6X and a guest beer – all either by the pint or the 4-pint jug, for the thirsty. Strongbow draught cider is also available. Meals are served at lunchtimes and in the evenings, at the usual times, seven days a week. This is a pub that is open all day. While children dining with their parents are welcome, no special provision is made for them as regards a play area. Dogs are only permitted in the garden.

Telephone: 01223 840295.

How to get there: Grantchester is 2 miles south-west of the centre of Cambridge. Take the Trumpington road from Cambridge, or the A10 from the south, and turn to the west at the village of Trumpington, to reach Grantchester in just under 1 mile. The Rupert Brooke is on the far side of the village, opposite the junction with Coton Road.

Parking: The Rupert Brooke has a large car park. Parking in the village is limited, though there are a few spaces near the church.

Length of the walk: 2½ miles. Map: OS Landranger sheet 154 Cambridge and Newmarket (inn GR 432557).

This short walk round the village starts across a meadow to join the cycle route between Grantchester and Cambridge and then continues through the village, passing the former mill and soon after crosses the river Cam by Brasley Bridge. Leaving the road, the path leads through a narrow belt of woodland to Byron's Pool, a secluded part of the Cam beside a weir from where the river water was diverted to power the mill, ¼ mile downstream. The return skirts the village along well-used farm tracks.

For those with plenty of time, a walk along the tarmac cycle route to the centre of Cambridge to view the river and the Backs (being the river frontage of many colleges), could be of interest but you would need to return the same way.

The Walk
From the Rupert Brooke go right along the road for 100 yards and turn right under an enormous horse chestnut tree onto the path signed 'Public Footpath to Cambridge 1'. Go through a geriatric wooden kissing-gate into the corner of a pasture, and follow the well-trodden path half-left across the field to the far left hedge. As you go you can see in the distance the skyline of Cambridge, and on

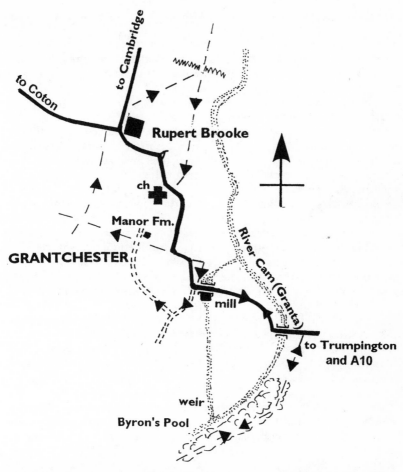

the right is the squat tower, topped with a tiny pyramidal spire, of the parish church of St Andrew and St Mary. You should reach the hedge where a tarmac path also meets it. This is a cycle path into Cambridge. Next to a metal gate is about the tiniest cattle grid imaginable. Do not go through the hedge but turn about and follow the tarmac path away from the hedge.

Now on your left is the meandering river Cam, 150 yards away. On the right, amongst Grantchester's thatched cottages, you can pick out the Rupert Brooke. Pass through the wooden kissing-gate with another minute cattle grid, and go straight ahead to reach a road opposite the churchyard wall.

The walk goes left here, but if you wish to divert to see the church, topped by its golden cockerel, now is the time to do so. The time on the church clock has been the subject of a series of letters to *The Times*.

Return to the road and in 100 yards swing right, and in a further 200 yards bend to the left. At the next bend to the right is the Old Vicarage. Immediately after that leave the road, going left along a leafy track with the Old Vicarage garden on your left, which takes you to the river again, where it has widened out to a pool into which water rushes from under the bridge.

To view this tranquil scene rest awhile on the bench there by the huge willow tree.

Go out to the road and turn left over the bridge past the Old Mill. Having crossed one arm of the river go on and in 300 yards cross another arm by Brasley Bridge. Continue past a group of cottages on the right and then immediately leave the road, turning right down a lane signed 'Byron's Pool'. A poet from an earlier era than Brooke was here. You are nearly into Trumpington now. You soon reach an open area, at the far side of which you go through a wooden kissing-gate and on along an earth path through light woodland. This eventually brings you to Byron's Pool, a quiet secluded part of the river.

Return to the road, turn left and walk back until you have just passed the Old Mill again. Where the road goes right, after the mill bridge, go left along a permissive path, a farm road which leads to Cantelupe Farm. In 150 yards go right on another permissive path, on a concrete farm road which leads round to the right towards Manor Farm. Just before the farmyard, at a junction of paths, turn left.

If for any reason the permissive paths are not available, continue after the bridge on the road round to the right, and then left, past the Old Vicarage, to the next bend to the right. Just by that corner, by a grassy area under a big lime tree opposite white Orchard House, go up past No 48, climbing, to the junction of paths by Manor Farm. With Manor Farm barns on your right go straight ahead.

Go up the hill on a concrete track until you come to a crossways of footpaths. Here go right on a slightly raised grassy path, through a wooden gate and on, now with a fence on the left and a post-and-rail fence on the right. Pass on the left a well-equipped play area and then the end of a close of old people's bungalows. Join a wide gravel drive, Burnt Close. At the end turn right and ahead of you is the Broadway and the Rupert Brooke once more.

18 Mepal
The Three Pickerels

As with so many of the more northern Cambridgeshire settlements, this small village of Mepal (rhyming with people) is in an isolated, lonely position. From Mepal, the adjacent village of Sutton is seen as standing on a hill. As this is merely on the 60 ft contour, it would never in other parts of Cambridgeshire rank as a hill, but here, in contrast to the low-lying fens, it is very noticeable. Mepal lies at the foot of this hill, on the road between Ely and Chatteris. It is on the bank of the New Bedford river, usually called the Hundred Foot Drain, which was built by Vermuyden, the engineer, an immigrant from Holland, in 1650. This is an almost straight canal between Earith and Denver, constructed to relieve flooding by bypassing the great loop of the Great Ouse through Ely. Vermuyden's earlier drainage canal, the Old Bedford river, runs parallel to and is about 250 yards away from the New Bedford river. There is more about this in the introduction to the Earith walk (No. 16).

The Three Pickerels stands above a long straight stretch of the New Bedford river. The river bank, set out with tables for warmer days, sparkles with daffodils in the spring. Inside the pub there is a warm welcome and good food. The public have the benefit of views of the river from inside the pub, as both the lounge bar and the restaurant have windows overlooking the water. The children can enjoy the garden area, but they will need supervision as the river is so close to the pub.

On the menu is 8 oz sirloin or fillet steak, with either Stilton or peppered sauce, venison pie, roast chicken and chips, tagliatelle carbonara, lasagne Romano, chicken tikka masala, lamb rogan josh and salmon en croûte. Death-by-Chocolate, crêpes with maple syrup and ice-cream, white chocolate bombshell, cassata Siciliana or tiramisu trifle, and yet more, are sure to tempt you to have a sweet. The real ales on offer change every so often, with several available at any one time, for instance, Tetley is one of those to enjoy. Gaymer's draught cider is on sale, too. The Three Pickerels is closed on Mondays. Meals are served from noon to 2 pm and from 6.30 to 11 pm. Dogs are not welcome.

Telephone: 01353 777777.

How to get there: Mepal is about 6 miles from Ely and just off the A142, Ely to Chatteris road. Turn off on the 'No Through Road' through the village. The Three Pickerels is at the end of this road.

Parking: There is plenty of parking in front of the pub.

Length of the walk: 3½ miles. Map: OS Landranger sheet 143 Ely, Wisbech and surrounding area (inn GR 440813).

The walk starts by going upstream alongside Vermuyden's New Bedford river. At Sutton Gault the route crosses the area between the New Bedford river and the Old Bedford river, which is known as the Hundred Foot Washes. In winter the land between the two rivers, or drains, is used to store the flood waters from the Great Ouse. The return is along the bank of the Old Bedford river. It is a quiet area, a haunt of wildlife.

The Walk

From the Three Pickerels pass by the side of the pub on a small tarmac footpath. Just beyond the pub grounds turn right over a stile into a meadow. Keep straight on beside the river. Walk under the road bridge, using the concrete strip just beside the bridge abutment. Should the river be high, you may have to go a few yards to the left to a stile and climb the embankment to cross the road, returning down the other side to another stile.

Keeping generally parallel to the river bank, cross two stiles in quick succession. The marshy area on the left here is known as Gault Hole. Cross yet another stile and then ignore the stile to the left, which leads to a footpath back to Mepal. Keep alongside the New Bedford river

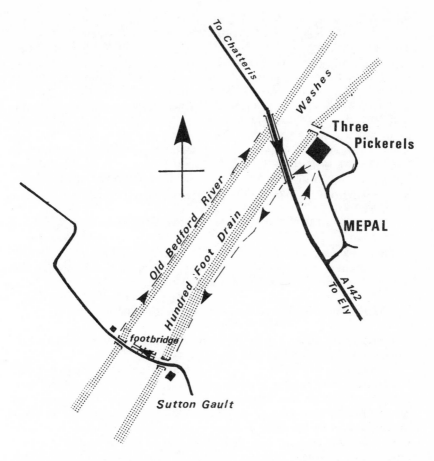

To Chatteris

Washes

Three Pickerels

Old Bedford River

MEPAL

Hundred Foot Drain

A 142

To Ely

footbridge

Sutton Gault

for about ½ mile and then go over a stile to reach a minor road at Sutton Gault, opposite the Anchor Inn.

Go right along the road to cross Gault Bridge. Just beyond the bridge, alongside the road, is a 200 yard long footbridge for pedestrians to use when the washes are covered with water. At the end of the footbridge cross a bridge over the Old Bedford river. There is a flood gate here which closes the road should heavy floods occur.

Immediately past the flood gate turn right over a stile, beside an old building. Follow a concrete track for 100 yards and at the end go right, up a flight of steps, and walk on the top of the river flood bank, crossing several stiles on the way. Beyond the river on the right are the washes. On the left at the bottom of the bank is a wide drainage ditch and flat fields beyond. Cross a stile leading to the main road. Here go left for a few yards round the end of the steel roadside crash barrier, then turn right along the road and go over the viaduct which crosses both rivers and the intervening washes. About 100 yards after the end of the bridge is a footpath sign on the left by a steel gate leading to a tarmac road. Go through a gap beside the gate, then turn sharp left and go over a stile into the corner of a meadow. Cross this meadow diagonally. There are groups of bushes in the field. Keep the bushes on your left and, in the middle of the field, a few yards from the bushes, stride a little ditch. At the diagonal corner of the field, close to the river on your left, go over the stile you crossed at the start of the walk and swing left on a tarmac path and you are back at the Three Pickerels.

Other local attractions: Nearby, on the Chatteris road, is the Mepal Outdoor Centre, catering for all manner of outdoor activities – windsurfing, Canadian canoeing, sailing, archery, trampolining and climbing. Open daily from 10 am to 5.30 pm. Telephone: 01354 692251.

19 Wisbech
The Tidnam's Tipple Inn

Wisbech is in the extreme north-east of Cambridgeshire. It is the main town of the Fens, that vast area south of the Wash which long ago was a great marsh. It was successfully drained and reclaimed in the 17th century by a consortium of adventurers, led by the Duke of Bedford, who put up capital for the drainage schemes in the expectation of new, rich agricultural land to be won from the erstwhile marsh. Today, Wisbech is a fine, interesting town. It has the navigable river Nene in its midst, lined with elegant buildings, and there are more Georgian buildings in the town centre. It is also a port. Along the banks of the river to the north of the town centre are wharfs and storage areas. The area surrounding Wisbech, known as the Strawberry Capital of England, specialises in fruit growing and market gardening.

The Tidnam's Tipple Inn at the Rose and Crown Hotel is reached from a carriage arch in the Market Place, which leads across a paved yard set out with tables and chairs. Tidnam's Tipple Inn is in what was once the coachman's area of a large 15th century coaching inn.

On the interesting menu is 'Field and Fowl', for those who cannot decide whether to have red or white meat. It consists of 4 oz prime rump steak and a quarter chargrilled chicken, served with a barbecue sauce. The 'Fensman' comprises diced pork, chopped celery, leek and diced apple in a pie. Lasagne, tuna and pasta bake and lamb cobbler are also available. There is a wide choice of sweets – 'Gourmet Tidnam's Treat', which is a chocolate shell filled with black cherries in port and kirsch, cherry ice-cream, topped with whipped cream and broken flake, Death-by-Chocolate, lemon lush pie, deep dish apple pie, fresh fruit salad and the usual range of puddings. The real ales are Greene King IPA, Adnams Bitter and Broadside, Ruddles County and a guest beer. Dry Blackthorn draught cider is also sold. The pub is open all day, from 10.30 am to 11 pm, on Thursdays and Saturdays, otherwise normal hours apply. Meals are served both at lunchtime and in the evenings seven days a week. Children can be served in the family room, or at the tables in the old coach yard. Dogs are only allowed in the courtyard, and must be on a lead.

Telephone: 01945 589800.

How to get there: Wisbech can be reached by the A47 Peterborough to King's Lynn road or the A1101 road from Ely. The inn is beside the Rose and Crown Hotel, which is at the north-west end of the Market Place, and is best approached from the public car park.

Parking: A large and convenient car park is just south of the church. Take the A1101 towards the town centre. Follow signs to the left for 'Town Centre Car Park'. Bear left in front of the church. To reach the inn from here leave the car park, keep left round the churchyard and enter the Market Place. Walk to the far end and you will see the Rose and Crown half-left.

Length of the walk: 3½ miles. Map: OS Landranger sheet 143 Ely, Wisbech and surrounding area (inn GR 462097).

Unlike most other walks in this book, this is a wander through the town. Starting in the market square, the walk explores the attractive Georgian streets. The route then follows the north bank of the river Nene, passing the front of the charming Peckover House, to a recreation ground and then returns to the river close to Elgood's Brewery. The walk continues along the Nene Way, eventually crossing a large sports ground to reach the river at the docks, to the north of the town. The return is alongside the river, across the town park and back to the market square.

The Walk
Leave the Tidnam's Tipple Inn and go straight ahead into the Market Place. Go to the far right corner, continue beside the churchyard and, opposite Stermyn Street, turn right under a wrought iron arch into the precincts of the church of St Peter and St Paul. Just after passing the

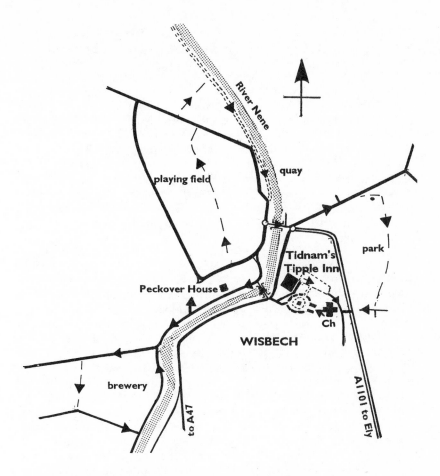

south porch, see on the left the Garden for the Blind.

As you pass the church, look back at the tower. You will see that it is almost separate from the church, abutting the north wall of the nave.

Continue straight past the church and then swing right up the broad stone steps leading to Museum Square, with its wide paved area and seats. Straight ahead is the castle. The present Regency building dates from 1816, but in 1087 a Norman castle stood here. In front of the castle gates go left into The Crescent, a part of the elliptical road around the castle and the gardens. After passing on the right a pair of large stone pillars, go right through a gap in iron railings into the small park behind the castle. Curve round to the right and leave the park to rejoin the road in Union Place. Turn left, and quite soon right into York Row.

You soon reach the tall Clarkson Memorial, reminiscent on a small scale of London's Albert Memorial, by the architect Sir George Gilbert Scott. Thomas Clarkson campaigned on behalf of slaves. From here you have a fine view of the river and the North and South Brinks.

From Bridge Street turn right over Town Bridge and go slightly right. Go into, and take a turn around, a long thin triangle which is the Old Market. Facing this are many old, mainly Georgian, buildings. Return to Town Bridge and bear right along North Brink, with the river on your left. While the houses are all different there is a unity about them, making a very attractive group on the river front. You will pass some bow-fronted houses, and later three-storey Peckover House, of 1722, now owned by the National Trust, behind which are 2 acres of delightful gardens. Continue along North Brink passing many elegant town houses.

Cross over Chapel Road and keep on along the North Brink. You will pass the buildings of Wisbech Grammar School, founded in 1379.

Reach Barton Road, turn right into it, and walk until the low brick wall topped with iron railings, bounding Woodcote Park, a new development, ends. Here turn left off the road into the corner of a playing field. Keep parallel to the park boundary on the left. Leave by a metal gate and meet a road, Magazine Lane. That this quiet road should have such a military sounding name is surprising, but there was an arsenal thereabouts in Napoleonic times. At its end, at a T-junction, once again meet North Brink. Turn left, with the flood defence wall on your right.

On the left is the high brick wall of Elgood's Brewery. Ale has been brewed here for almost 200 years. The main brewery is Georgian.

Pass the end of Barton Road and when you reach Chapel Road turn left. At the road junction curve round to the right on the footway, beneath the high brick perimeter garden wall of Peckover House. Cross the road, with playing fields on your left, and continue until you reach the car park for Peckover House. Turn left immediately before the car park, where the path is signed 'Nene Way'. Walk across the paved area for 20 yards and go left into the playing field, and immediately right, under lime, horse chestnut and silver birch trees. Walk along the edge of the playing field. At the end of the first field, close to the right edge, cross a ditch and continue, following the beech hedge on your right.

When the hedge goes right, go right with it, and then left, to continue in the same direction as previously, along the playing field boundary, with mature trees on the right. At the end of that second field cross a shallow ditch by a culvert and continue as before. At the end of the playing fields the path continues in the same direction, at the edge of an urban area. Swing right a little to walk between elder trees and in 100 yards go through a gap in a wooden fence to join a road by a telephone box and the Oak Brewery. Go left along the road, and cross the busy road by the pelican crossing opposite the West End Inn.

84

Walk across the car park of the inn and continue on a path, then cross a grassy play area and go on until you reach a road and the concrete river wall. On the opposite side of the river are many wharfs. Turn right (the Nene Way goes left here) and walk alongside the river by West Parade. When the road divides, keep up, by the river, passing a series of twelve cottages. The river wall is punctured at intervals by flood gates, reminding one of how vulnerable to flooding this area still is.

Rejoin the road and walk along to Freedom Bridge.

Cross the river Nene by the bridge and passing a huge roundabout on the right, keep straight on along Lynn Road. Pass De Havilland Road on the left and immediately cross the road at the pelican crossing.

To the left, on a little knoll beside a petrol station stands the eight-storey high tower of a former windmill. Some 100 yards beyond the mill turn right alongside Park Avenue and enter the park. There are many fine specimen trees here. Wander round the park, keeping the park boundary on your left pass the children's play area, the tennis court and the bowling green. At the far corner of the park go out, passing iron gates, and turn right along William Road.

At the end of the road continue on a narrow snicket which leads directly to a pelican crossing over a dual-carriageway. Cross the road and go straight on towards the church. Turn right in front of the church onto a road which will lead you back to the market square and the start.

Other local attractions: Peckover House, now owned by the National Trust, was once the home of a wealthy local Quaker banker. The elaborate, elegant interior, makes a visit well worth while. The 2 acre Victorian walled garden is full of interesting and rare plants. Both house and gardens are open to the public from the end of March till the end of October on Wednesdays, Sundays and bank holiday Mondays from 2 pm till 5.30 pm. The gardens alone are open from end of March to the end of October on Saturdays, Mondays and Tuesdays from 2 pm till 5.30 pm. On certain days there are 'Walks with the Gardener': Telephone: 01945 583463.

Wisbech and Fenland Museum contains much of general interest about the area. There are sections on geology, fishing, wildfowling, drainage, topography and the local woad industry, and there are displays about the port of Wisbech. The life of Thomas Clarkson, the anti-slavery campaigner who was born in Wisbech, where his father was headmaster of the Grammar School, is featured. Entrance is free, but the museum relies on voluntary contributions. It is open from Tuesday to Saturday, April to September from 10 am to 5 pm, and from October to March from 10 am to 4 pm.

20 Whittlesford
The Tickell Arms

Whittlesford village lies among the meadows beside the river Cam, which flows northward to Cambridge. Although a mere 6 miles from Cambridge, the village is small and quiet. The main roads of the district seem to have passed it by, whereas, by contrast, Sawston, on the opposite side of the Cam, has developed into a thriving village.

The Tickell Arms is a somewhat unusual pub in the main street just north of the crossroads, where the fine half-timbered Guildhall stands, with an attractive white pigeon loft set against its north wall. If it wasn't for the sign at the road side, no one would realise that the detached, dark blue-painted house standing well back from the road, behind an iron railing, is, in fact, the village pub. The striking fenestration is also to be seen in another house in the village, in Church Lane, passed on the last lap of the walk. The attractive pub has a covered outdoor eating and drinking area to one side, which looks out onto a large formal pond with a fountain. Inside, in both the spacious public areas, are marble fireplaces with welcoming large log fires on cool days. Many of the tables are in keeping with those in a stately home and give a touch of elegant living to the visit.

The food here (around 95% of it home-made) has to be tasted to be believed. On the menu are such starters as carrot and basil soup, smoked duck breast, scallops in lobster sauce and Geschnetzetles – beef cut into thin strips and served in a lemon sauce. The main courses include locally smoked Scottish salmon, lamb's kidneys, prawn and almond curry, roast duck breast with red wine, redcurrant or orange sauce, Hungarian goulash, fresh salmon with sauce thermidor, Andalusian chicken, pheasant casserole, smoked trout and salad. Finally, among the sweets on offer are crème brûlée, meringue chestnut cream, Mississippi mud pie and chocolate fudge cheesecake. The real ales served are Adnams and Greene King Abbot. There is Strongbow draught cider, too. The pub is open and meals are available during the usual hours, but it is closed all day on Mondays. However, it is open on bank holiday Mondays, and it then closes on the Tuesday following. Children over the age of twelve are welcome, as are well-behaved dogs.

Telephone: 01223 833128.

How to get there: Whittlesford can be reached from the A505 main road, which runs from the A11, south-west of Newmarket, to Royston and beyond. Turn north off the A505 on a minor road about 1 mile east of the interchange with the M11 near Duxford airfield. The Tickell Arms is in the main street about 100 yards north of the green. Note: the turning to take is west of the railway. The road to Whittlesford station, east of the railway line, will not take you to the village.

Parking: While actually in the pub you can park on the forecourt, but the gates may be shut out of pub hours. There are many side roads where parking is allowed.

Length of the walk: 3 miles. Map: OS Landranger sheet 154 Cambridge and Newmarket (inn GR 472483).

This short walk crosses the watermeadows beside the river Cam to the large village of Sawston, from where the return passes the former Whittlesford Mill. Almost all this walk is along firm tracks and tarmac footpaths and is likely to be comfortable and easy to walk in all weathers. Two stiles and a short length of cross-field path can be avoided if you like, by a small diversion along a road.

The Walk

From the Tickell Arms go left and walk away from the village. In 200 yards, at a footpath sign to Sawston, go right through a pedestrian gate beside steel gates onto a wide tarmac footpath which leads to Whittlesford church.

When you come to the churchyard turn left, still on a tarmac path, at

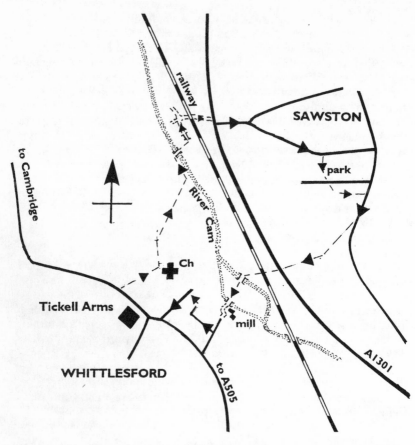

first between fences and later between hedges. The path crosses a dry ditch on a large footbridge 12 yards long. You can see, over to the left, a paper mill. The narrow tarmac footpath is on a low bank between two arable fields, leading straight to the bank of the river Granta. Turn left along the bank for 100 yards, then turn right and cross the river by a steel bridge.

Cross another steel bridge close to an electricity transformer station. Then turn left, crossing a ditch by a brick culvert, and continue on a tarmac track parallel to the railway. On the left, about 10 yards beyond the brick culvert, are two black cylinders set vertically in the ground, being the tops of the National Rivers Authority's water quality monitoring boreholes. You come to a factory access road. Turn right and cross the railway by an automatic level crossing and then, almost immediately, cross with great care the dual-carriageway, and go down

Mill Lane opposite, into Sawston. At the next junction keep right, still in Mill Lane.

Pass Chestnut Close on the right and Sawston Fire Station. When you reach the recreation ground go right and follow the boundary on the right. Leave the sports field at the corner, close to a lime tree, on a narrow cinder footpath leading to a road, Common Lane.

To avoid two stiles and cross-field path, turn left along Common Lane. When you reach the T-junction in the village turn right. Pass the White Lion, and the Black Bull next door. Here you rejoin the main route.

If not taking the diversion, cross the stile opposite into a pasture and turn left, making for the internal corner of the field behind a house, then continue parallel to the garden fences on the left. In the corner of the field cross a stile and go straight through the Black Bull pub car park to Sawston's main street. Turn right to pass in front of the Black Bull.

In 150 yards, opposite Prince William Way, on the left, go right on a tarmac footpath, signed to Whittlesford. Cross a bridge over a watercourse. The path is fenced, with a field on the right and gardens on the left. Join another tarmac path coming in from the left behind you. *Carefully* cross the main road and continue, still on a tarmac path, and in 100 yards cross the railway with care. It is a STOP-LOOK-LISTEN crossing through two pedestrian gates. The railway line is straight here and you would easily see a train coming.

The tarmac path continues. Cross a footbridge over the Cam. Through the trees on the right you can see Whittlesford church. After the bridge the fenced path continues between pastures. This leads into a narrow tarmac road. After a white house on the right you cross a bridge with brick parapets. Look over the parapet to see the mill stream. On the left there is the three-storey former mill building, now converted to another use. A sign says 'University of Cambridge – Hamilton Kerr Institute'.

Pass William Westley's Church of England primary school, and when you come to the village green go right along The Lawn. The green contains a children's play area, hard tennis courts and a cricket pitch and pavilion. At the end of the green the road turns right for a few yards to the head of a cul-de-sac. Near the end turn left on a tarmac path (you are going towards the church) until you reach a road, another cul-de-sac, leading to the church. Turn left on this road, with an old brick wall on the right. Pass on the left a thatched house with very decorative windows, similar to those at the pub.

Come out to a road by the war memorial. Turn right on North Road and you will reach the Tickell Arms.

Other local attractions: The Imperial War Museum at Duxford is about 1 mile south of Whittlesford, alongside the A505.

21 Purls Bridge
The Ship Inn

This area is the heartland of the Fens. It is serene and seemingly far from the brash cities and a fair distance from any bustling market towns. Flat it may be, but it has its own unique and lonely beauty, an antidote to the hectic everyday town rush. You will search in vain for the bridge at Purls Bridge. Purl is Old English for a rivulet or stream. Before 1630 when Vermuyden cut the Old Bedford river and all the other many long, straight drainage ditches, it is thought that there must have been a stream somewhere near the present site of the pub, and crossed by a track. Hence Purls Bridge. You will notice that fenland roads are mostly higher than the surrounding countryside. As the land was drained the peat shrank and the level of the fields dropped (see Introduction).

The Ship is a light and airy, friendly pub right on the waterfront on the lonely stretch of road that leads only to the RSPB's Ouse Washes reserve and to Welches Dam, less than a mile further along the road. The river, in the days before the railways took over their trade, was in constant use by barges plying up and down, bringing much custom to the landlords of the three riverside alehouses which used to be clustered here. The Ship was built in the 1820s, in the heyday of barge traffic. The

Three Fishes by Welches Dam, now a cottage, was once a pub. Now the custom for the Ship comes from those who seek a quiet spot with good food, amid tranquil surroundings. The entertainment inside the pub is also of the soothing, peaceful variety. There are board games supplied and a small library of books to read by the windows looking out over the river – no fruit machines or computer games! Outside there are picnic tables overlooking the river, and an area for children.

There is a comprehensive menu to choose from: home-made soup, prawn cocktail, garlic mushrooms, crispy-coated baby corn cobs, T-bone or fillet or rump steak with red wine sauce, Ship Inn chicken, Hawaiian gammon, home-made boeuf bourguignonne, home-made beef casserole, lasagne verdi and several vegetarian dishes. Friday's 'Supergrill' sounds gargantuan – rump steak, sausage, pork, lamb chop, bacon, burger, liver and mushrooms. How about a banana boat or apple pie to round off the meal? Greene King real ales are on sale. So is Scrumpy Jack draught cider. The pub is closed on Mondays. Meals are served every other day of the week, both at lunchtime and in the evenings. Dogs are not welcome.

Telephone: 01354 680578.

How to get there: The Ship at Purls Bridge lies near the end of a long, long cul-de-sac, 1 mile from the isolated village of Manea, which itself is 6 miles north-east of Chatteris. Reach Chatteris on the A141 Huntingdon to Wisbech road, or the A142 from Ely. Take the B1098 and in 2½ miles cross a bridge over the Forty Foot Drain and bear right for Manea. In the village turn right for Purls Bridge.

Parking: The Ship has its own car park. The RSPB has a car park (Trust the Motorist), ½ mile down the road at Welches Dam.

Length of the walk: 4 miles. Map: OS Landranger sheet 143 Ely, Wisbech and surrounding area (inn GR 478869).

This walk starts alongside the Old Bedford river and at the edge of the Ouse Washes RSPB bird reserve. In winter the washes are often covered with flood water and are a nationally important refuge for ducks, geese and other wading birds. The route continues to where the wide, straight drainage canal, called the Forty Foot Drain, intersects with the Old Bedford river at Welches Dam. A few years ago volunteers of the Inland Waterways Association, with the help of the National Rivers Authority, restored the old lock, which now enables boats to move between the canals of the north and west of Cambridgeshire and the Bedford river.

The walk crosses arable fields to the outskirts of Manea before returning to Purls Bridge.

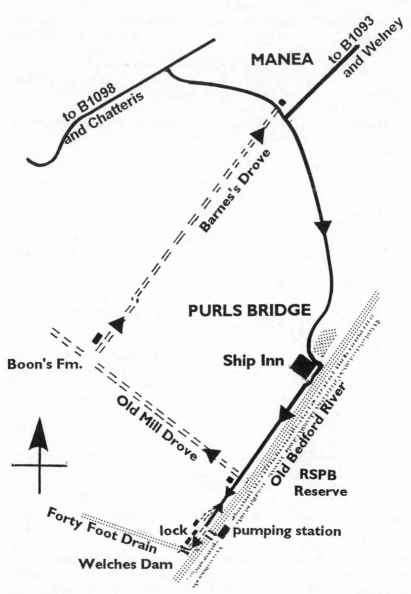

The Walk

From the Ship go right, along the bank of the Old Bedford river. On the opposite side of the river are the hides of the RSPB's Ouse Washes reserve. In ½ mile pass a large pumping station on the opposite side of the river and, shortly after, a bridge. On the right, just opposite the bridge, is a car park and RSPB visitors' centre for the Ouse Washes nature reserve.

Go beyond the bridge for a few hundred yards to see Welches Dam. The last cottage on the right, called the Three Fishes, is an attractive small brick-built building with dormer windows. Have a look at Welches Dam and notice the plate, 'Welches Dam Lock. Restored by Inland Waterways Association. Reopened on April 6th 1991 in memory of Sir Geoffrey De Freitas formerly President of the Inland Waterways Association'.

Retrace your steps, walking on the road at the foot of the river bank. About 400 yards beyond the visitors' centre, come to a low, black weather-boarded pumping station, beside which is a 'Bridleway' sign. Turn left onto a cart track known as Old Mill Drove and follow this track for about ¾ mile, alongside a drainage ditch on the left which gets increasingly narrow. After passing the ends of five cross-ditches on the right, come to abandoned farm buildings with a few trees behind them.

At the derelict farm go straight on past the end of the sixth drainage ditch on the right, parallel with the others, then turn right onto Barnes's Drove, a cart track alongside the drainage ditch, to pass the old farmhouse on the left.

Continue along Barnes's Drove for 1½ miles. You are crossing fields of rich jet-black peaty soil, good for growing all sorts of crops, for example, onions, carrots and corn. Over to the right you can see the tower of Ely cathedral.

All the way along this track you have been walking towards a white house. When you reach the road opposite it, turn right. In 100 yards do not turn to Manea but keep straight on and walk back to the Ship.

Other local attractions: The Royal Society for the Protection of Birds' reserve at Welches Dam (established in 1964) is part of the Ouse Washes – the largest area of regularly flooded washland in Great Britain. It is one of the most important wintering grounds for birds in Europe, and thousands of wildfowl feed there in the winter. The Ouse Washes are a vast storage area for the flood waters of the Great Ouse. They were created in the mid-17th century, between the Old and the New Bedford rivers. They stretch for about 19 miles and cover over 5,000 acres, the RSPB owning 1,700 acres. Display boards record which species have been seen recently. The visitors' centre is open from 10 am to 5 pm at weekends all year, except public holidays and Christmas and Boxing Day. Telephone: 01767 680551.

22 Stretham
The Lazy Otter

Stretham is a fenland village at the southern edge of what was the Isle of Ely, and close to the river Great Ouse. A parish leaflet explains that the name Stretham means 'home on the street' and refers to it being on Akeman Street, the Roman road, now the A10, from Cambridge towards the Wash. This flat fenland, as with much of north-east Cambridgeshire, is dependent upon good and adequate drainage and requires large pumping stations. The Stretham Old Engine House, containing a steam boiler, beam engine and large scoop wheel is a fine and historic example of such a station.

The Lazy Otter is a charming, isolated pub in an idyllic riverside setting. From one of the several interconnected dining areas there are wide views down across the grassed outdoor seating area by the river, to the boats tied up at the Lazy Otter's berths, and to the passing craft on the broad waterway. The lawns provide a good play area for children, but the young will need supervision beside the water. The Lazy Otter has been a pub since 1603, though it was called the Royal Oak at one time. Inside, as you might expect, there are many paintings of otters around the walls.

On the menu are 'Megaburgers' and chips, ham, eggs and chips, baked vegetable loaf, home-made lasagne, fish and chips, cannelloni verdi filled with ricotta cheese and spinach, 10 oz gammon steak with either peach, pineapple or fried egg, fresh English rump steak and a 'Mixed Grill for the Big Appetite' – steak, gammon, sausage, liver, lamb chop, fried egg, mushrooms, tomato, onion rings, chips and peas. If you can contemplate anything to follow after that, there is a special menu of exotic ice-creams and a range of sweets. The children's menu includes sphagetti shapes with meat balls. Marston's Pedigree Bitter, Greene King Abbot and IPA and Rayments Special Bitter are the real ales served. Dry Blackthorn draught cider is on sale too. This is a pub that is open all day, every day, from 11 am to 11 pm on weekdays and the permitted hours on Sundays. In winter meals are served from 12 noon until 2.30 pm and from 6 pm until 10 pm, while in summer they are available from 12 noon right through until 10 pm. On Wednesdays there is live music at the Lazy Otter. Dogs are not welcome inside the building, as food is served throughout the pub.

Telephone: 01353 649780.

How to get there: Stretham is about 4 miles south of Ely, on the main A10 Cambridge to Ely road. The Lazy Otter is 1 mile south of Stretham, on a short loop road to the east of the A10, beside the river Great Ouse.

Parking: The pub has a large car park.

Length of the walk: 6 miles. Map: OS Landranger sheets 154 Cambridge and Newmarket and 143 Ely, Wisbech and surrounding area (inn GR 501722).

From Stretham Ferry Bridge, beside the Lazy Otter, the walk follows the river Great Ouse, also known as the Old West river, passing the Stretham Old Engine House, almost as far as the confluence with the river Cam. The return is across farmland to the village of Stretham, and back along the north bank of the Great Ouse.

The Walk

From the Lazy Otter go left along the road and cross the Stretham Ferry Bridge over the river Great Ouse. Then turn left, over a stile, to walk along the river bank, with the river on the left. Teazles grow abundantly along both sides of the river. You will soon see the engine house, a tall brick building with a slender chimney, ahead.

After a mile on the river bank, and having crossed several stiles en route, reach a roadbridge across the river. Do not cross the bridge but keep straight on for about 100 yards to the Stretham Old Engine House,

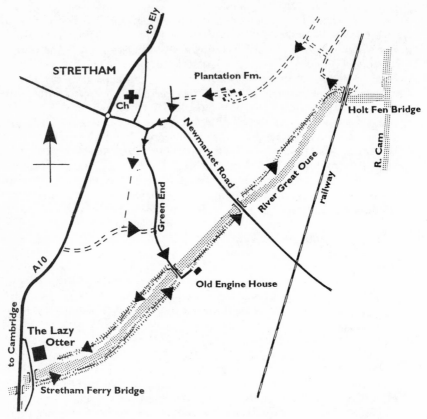

which is well worth a visit. Continue on the river bank for a further ½ mile. The village of Stretham can be seen half-left, and you will reach the A1123, Newmarket Road, just by a bridge.

Cross the river on the roadbridge and go right at a footpath sign to continue on the opposite bank of the river. Cross a ditch by a sluice gate and continue, still on the river's flood bank. Half-left you may see the tower of Ely cathedral. In about ½ mile you reach a railway bridge, Holt Fen Bridge.

If you have time, you can extend the walk by going under the railway and following the river Great Ouse for a further ¼ mile to its confluence with the river Cam, where, on the opposite side of the river, lies the Fish and Duck, a lonely and isolated pub. Retrace your steps back under the railway bridge.

To continue the walk, just clear of the bridge, go over a stile, off the flood bank. Do not go under the railway but keep round to the left. Take a farm track, beside several water-loving trees along a 20 ft wide grassy swathe, with a deep ditch on either side, back towards the village of Stretham. In 200 yards the track swings round to the right.

The path shown on the definitive map from this point is not usable because of missing bridges, however the parish has arranged and waymarked with white arrows a permissive diversion. Follow the farm track as it swings round to the right. In 200 yards turn left along a cart track and in a further 200 yards go left along a tarmac farm road to Plantation Farm. Go diagonally across the yard and take the concrete farm drive.

The drive leads into a road. In 50 yards turn left at a T-junction. Pass Meadow Croft on the left and swing round to the right to the main Newmarket road. Turn right along the main road. As you pass, look into Chapel Street and see the attractive small tree, a variety of maple, outside the former chapel.

Take the first turning to the left, called Green End, where a sign says 'To Stretham Old Engine House'. At a footpath sign, just past No 14B, a bungalow, turn right on a narrow footpath, with a ditch on the right. After crossing a plank bridge turn left along a footpath. Cross a two-sleeper bridge and carry on, with a ditch and a hedge on the left. The path continues beside the ditch on the left, with a number of bridges on the way. The footpath leads out, at right-angles, to a grassy cart track, called Middle Common Drove. Turn left, out to the road, and turn right towards the engine house.

When you reach the river bridge turn right along the bank, with the river Great Ouse on the left, back to the Lazy Otter, a mile away.

Other local attractions: The Stretham Old Engine, now disused, with its massive 37 ft diameter wooden scoop wheel, could raise a phenomenal 30 tons of water from the land drains, and empty it into the river, for each revolution. It is a fine example of a land drainage steam engine, dating from 1831. It is open daily from the beginning of April until the end of September from 11.30 am to 5 pm, and during October at weekends only. Telephone: 01353 649210.

㉓ Clayhithe
The Bridge Hotel

The Bridge Hotel, originally built in 1756, is a riverside pub on the banks of the Cam. In the grounds, under the shade of a gnarled old willow tree, is a red-painted gypsy type of caravan, just such a one as Toad might have travelled in on his adventures by the river. In the lounge there are many watercolours, hunting horns, brass measures and other brasses to enliven the walls. As well as the thickly-carpeted, pleasant lounge, with views of the river, there is a large restaurant, resplendent in light natural wood with pink upholstery, napery and lampshades. A family room and outdoor play area are both available and children are welcome.

On the menu are mouth-watering dishes such as 'Chef's Own Lasagne', chicken Kiev, gammon steak and egg or pineapple, roast chicken, bacon and sausage, calamares, chilli and dip, rump steak, tomato and mushrooms, vegetable lasagne and sweet and sour pork. These can be followed by lemon meringue pie, home-made apple pie, chocolate gâteau or peach melba. Meals are served both at lunchtimes and in the evenings every day of the week. The real ales on offer are Adnams Broadside and Elgood's Cambridge Bitter.

Telephone: 01223 860252.

How to get there: Clayhithe is 3 miles north-east of Cambridge. Travel eastbound on the Cambridge bypass (A14) take the slip road to the B1047. Go through Horningsea and in about 1 mile reach Clayhithe Bridge. The Bridge Hotel is just beyond the bridge on the right.

Parking: The car park at the pub is large.

Length of the walk: 2½ miles. Map: OS Landranger sheet 154 Cambridge and Newmarket (inn GR 502644).

This short walk follows the river Cam downstream to Bottisham lock. The river is used by pleasure craft traversing the intricate series of rivers and man-made waterways through this part of Cambridgeshire. Passing a large drainage pumping station, the walk leaves the river beside the Bottisham Lode, a drainage channel, and returns to the start across rich arable land.

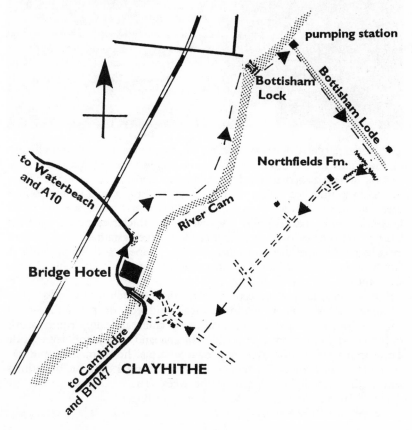

The Walk

Leave the Bridge Hotel and go right, away from the river along the road towards Waterbeach, carefully watching out for traffic. Where the road bends sharply round to the left, use the old gravel track, a kind of service road, passing the Motorboat Club and the Sailing Club, to go round the bend. Having rejoined the road, in 100 yards at a footpath sign, go right along a path on a wide raised bank, with a deep ditch on the left. Go through a gate and turn sharp right, then through another pedestrian gate. Continue on the path through a rough area, with a hedge on the right, and through a third pedestrian gate which leads in another 20 yards to the river bank.

Go left along the river bank, with the Cam on your right. You will soon pass the Sailing Club's signal station. Keep along the river bank for about ½ mile, crossing stiles on your route. Pass a small boat basin. Keep on top of the bank through another pedestrian gate which leads to a few houses and a road at Bottisham Lock. Immediately after the gate, turn right to go over the sluice gates and cross the lock by a bridge.

Leave the well-tended grassy surroundings of the lock through a gate and go left, still following the Cam, but now walking on the opposite bank, with the river on your left. About 200 yards ahead, there is a large pumping station. Immediately before the building, turn right over a stile and walk beside a wide drainage ditch on the left.

At the end of the field go over a stile without a footpiece or through a gate, if it is openable, into a narrow long pasture between a drainage ditch on the left and a hedge on the right. Halfway along this field, close to a solitary willow tree, go right over another stile without a footpiece and continue on a headland path, with a hedge on the right.

Go through a gate and continue in the same direction, still with a hedge on the right. Skirt round some timber cattle pens on the right and turn right through a gate, on the right, onto a farm drive and continue in the same general direction as before, now on a concrete drive. Keep to the drive when it turns right and, soon after, turn left onto a gravel farm road. When the gravel drive makes a sharp turn go straight ahead across a field. At the far side you come to a gravel farm road at right angles. Turn right and go towards the barns. The farm road takes you through a farmyard, with barns to the left and to the right.

After the farm, where the main farm track goes half-left, you swing slightly right, along a gravel track with grass in the middle, keeping to the right of a large house, dated 1842, with strange and fancy Dutch gables on all four sides. At the river bank bear left, in sight of the Bridge Hotel. At the road turn right and go over Clayhithe Bridge, built in 1939, back to the start.

Little Wilbraham
The Hole in the Wall

The Wilbrahams are a pair of villages 5 miles east of Cambridge. Like many settlements in this county they stand on land at the edge of the fens. To the north-west of Little Wilbraham lies the flat Little Wilbraham Fen, below the 30 ft contour and crossed by the Little Wilbraham river flowing into Quy Water and thence to the Cam. In contrast, the land to the south and east is rounded chalky downs rising to 300 ft in height. Although close to the city, with two major traffic roads within two miles, the villages retain their rural charm.

The Hole in the Wall inn is a delightful timber-framed pub dating from 1462, which is 30 years before Christopher Columbus discovered America. The pub was, many years ago, an off-licence selling beer from a hole in the wall, to farm workers and others who presented their small wooden barrels at the hole to be filled and taken back to the fields. The landlord has some of those old barrels in the bar. Inside the pub, right in the corner, the now blocked up hole can still be seen. Outside, behind the big tree, the hole has been rendered over.

In the main part of the inn, where a log fire burns in the large grate on chilly days, meals are served. An old barn, adjoining the inn, has been converted into an attractive restaurant open in the evening. The

101

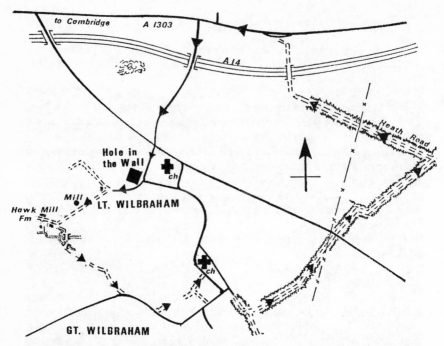

food served here is excellent, most of it home-cooked, and includes, among many other delights, pork à la crème, sirloin steak with either mushroom sauce or blue vein sauce, steak and Guinness pie, man-sized mixed grill, a 1 lb T-bone steak and half a roast duck, all bones removed, with orange sauce. Rum and coffee gâteau, lemon meringue pie, apple pie, blackberry and apple crumble, sherry trifle, brandy cheesecake topped with cherries or profiteroles are offered as mouth-watering sweets. Children are welcome to dine with their parents. The real ales on offer are Marston's Pedigree Bitter, John Smith's, Rayments Special Bitter and Greene King IPA. Meals are served at lunchtime and in the evenings from Tuesday through to Saturday, and also at Sunday lunchtime. The inn is closed on Sunday evening and all day Monday. Dogs are not permitted in the inn.

Telephone: 01223 812282.

How to get there: Leave the A14 at the grade-separated interchange on the east side of Cambridge, signed 'Burwell and Newmarket' from the west and 'Burwell and Cambridge' from the east. Follow the A1303 towards Newmarket for about 1 mile and then turn right for the Wilbrahams. In another mile, at a crossroads, turn right and in about 300 yards you will find the Hole in the Wall on the right.

Parking: There is plenty of parking at the inn.

Length of the walk: 7 miles (or there is the option of a short cut, reducing it to 3 miles). Map: OS Landranger sheet 154 Cambridge and Newmarket (inn GR 543585).

This walk divides naturally into two parts. It starts through the village of Little Wilbraham and goes to the edge of the fen, passing the former windmill. After crossing the Little Wilbraham river the route follows a green lane to Great Wilbraham, then continues over chalky farmland, in marked contrast to the fields seen earlier. Here the walk follows tracks which are along wide, straight lanes between hedges about 15 yards apart across gently rolling downs. These broad ways were probably laid out as drove roads at a time when the land hereabouts was used for sheep rearing. They ·could easily accommodate flocks of sheep being driven between their pasture, the farm and the market.

If you want a shorter walk, you can return from Great Wilbraham by road (a total circuit of 3 miles).

The Walk
Leave the pub, going right along the High Street, signed 'No Through Road'. Pass Orchard Close on the right and on the left, Manor House, a white four-bay farmhouse. Opposite Manor Close bear left in front of three small detached single-storey cottages, along Mill Road. A sign says 'Private Road to Windmill and Hawk Mill Farm/Footpath only'. Pass the windmill, now converted into a dwelling, on the right, and in 200 yards reach a bend where the rough road turns right.

At the present time the public right of way goes right, along the road, for 150 yards to Hawk Mill Farm, where it turns left through the garden to follow the edge of a ditch. However, there is a proposal, supported by the parish council, to divert the right of way, and the farmer has given permission for people to use the proposed new route.

Hence, following the proposed diversion, turn left off the road at the bend and follow a deep ditch on the right. Keep beside the stream as it turns right and in 100 yards go straight ahead to rejoin the right of way over a bridge crossing a shallow ditch. Unusually, the water in the deep ditch you have been following goes through a pipe under the shallow ditch to continue beyond the bridge. Keep beside the deep ditch on your right for about 50 yards.

Turn right, crossing a second bridge, followed by a stile. There is a sign saying 'Grazing cattle/Do not annoy'. Beyond the stile turn half-left, skirting a small pond on the left and going in the direction of a wooden electricity pole. Make for a waymark on a post in the middle of the field. At the waymark you are on a grassy cart track in this rough pasture. Keep on the track, passing several bushes.

Leave the field by a stile beside an iron gate into a green lane. In just over ¼ mile come out to a road and turn left. You will eventually reach the edge of Great Wilbraham. Pass a row of houses on the left and then turn left into Toft Lane. Pass a vehicle turning area and keep straight ahead, on a tarmac footpath. You can see, half-left, the church at Great Wilbraham. At a T-junction of tracks, near some dwellings, bear slightly left, still on Toft Lane, which leads out to a road opposite a children's play area and the Great Wilbraham village green.

For the shorter walk, turn left along the village street, following the road for about ¾ mile. Where the road bends right go straight on to reach the Hole in the Wall in 300 yards.

For the longer walk, turn right at the children's playground and walk south along the village street. When the main road makes a right turn to Fulbourn go left into High Street, and in 30 yards turn right into Butts Lane. Go past some large metal gates and you are on a gravel cart track between hedges 15 yards apart. In about 100 yards or so you come to a Y-junction of tracks. Keep to the track that curves round to the left. The one swinging to the right is a permissive path.

You are on a 15 yard wide driftway, with hedges on both sides. In about ½ mile go under grid lines and then cross straight over a road, and continue on this wide driftway. The track snakes 100 yards to the right and then left again, in the same direction as before. In about ½ mile you reach an intersection of two wide driftways. Here you turn left onto a track called Heath Road. Between the hedges, still 15 yards apart, there are overhead electric cables on twin poles. In about 200 yards, in the hedge on the left, is an old Ordnance Survey trig pillar with its top knocked off. These pillars are usually sited at high points with all-round views – this one is no exception.

On the left in the middle of a field is a tiny water tank on a gantry about 20 ft high. The tank is too small for irrigation or as a public water supply. Perhaps it is a relic of a time when this land was used for livestock rearing.

Go under the grid lines and in ½ mile join a roadway which leads up over a bridge across the A14 dual-carriageway. Keep on the road and come out to a large layby and bear left, along a wide verge beside the Newmarket to Cambridge road (A1303). Go left at the next road on the left, to Little Wilbraham. Cross the dual-carriageway again by another bridge and walk straight on down the road. In ½ mile at a crossroads, go straight on and reach the Hole in the Wall, your starting point, in 300 yards.

25 Hildersham
The Pear Tree

Hildersham and Linton lie in the valley of the river Granta, a tributary of the Cam which flows north through Cambridge to the Ouse. The Ordnance Survey maps of the area indicate some duplication of names because the river Cam, both upstream and downstream of its junction with the Linton Granta, is also called the Granta. To make confusion worse, another tributary of the Cam, which flows from the west towards Grantchester, is also called the Cam. Rivey Hill, on the top of which is a water tower, stands prominently overlooking Linton, whilst a mile further north an ancient trackway, known as Roman Road, crosses the chalk downland. Because of the proximity of the downs, there are several flint-faced cottages in the vicinity.

The Pear Tree is a charming, immaculate pub, full of surprises. Should you ponder the purpose of the chains hanging from the ceiling you will learn that at one time tables hung from them. Did the tables not swing all over the place? No, there were also chains to anchor them to the floor! The landlord has an enviable collection of framed diplomas on the wall. In fact, he lectures on vegetarian cookery and on hygiene, and has published a booklet of vegetarian recipes.

The menu is wide ranging. Vegetarian dishes, such as mixed nut loaf with cheese and tomato layers and vegetables, black-eye bean bourguignonne with rice and salad, red kidney beans with ginger and chilli, and asparagus and almond terrine, are served. For the non-vegetarians there is pork Napoleon, fillet, sirloin and rump steaks in various sizes and grey mullet fillet with tomato sauce and vegetables. Under elevens' choices include fish fingers, pork chipolatas and chicken fillets, all with chips and baked beans. Next on the menu come chocolate fudge cake, treacle tart, coconut and apricot sponge, pecan pie, coffee and walnut pudding, chocolate brandy mousse, Pear Tree pavlova and banana split. And that's just a selection! Such real ales as Greene King IPA and Abbot are served. Dry Blackthorn draught cider is also sold. The pub is open during the usual hours and meals are served at lunchtimes and in the evenings seven days a week. Last orders are taken 1½ hours before closing time. In the garden there are tables and chairs, and an aviary beyond. A bouncy castle is provided in summer. Children, if 'good-mannered' are also welcome in the bar.

Telephone: 01223 891680.

How to get there: Hildersham is just off the A604 Cambridge to Colchester road, 2 miles east of the roundabout at the intersection with the A11. The Pear Tree is on the minor road through the village.

Parking: There is some parking in front of the pub, and more in the car park up behind the pub.

Length of the walk: 6 miles. Map: OS Landranger sheet 154 Cambridge and Newmarket (inn GR 543484).

The route starts with a climb to the higher downland, to walk the ancient Roman Road. The walk continues on the Icknield Way over Rivey Hill, with fine views of the surrounding country, descending to the village of Linton. The return is along the valley beside the river Granta. You will pass waymarks indicating that some of the walk is along the Roman Road Circular Walk.

At the edge of the Linton Recreation Ground is an unusual stile, a clapper stile, which comprises three horizontal rails each supported by a single spindle and kept horizontal by a wooden counterweight at the end. To operate the clapper stile, a user must push down on the free end of the top rail and stride the rails. When released, the rails return to their horizontal position with a clapping sound, thus preventing stock from escaping from the field.

The Walk
From the Pear Tree go left towards the river. Immediately before the bridge go right at a footpath sign, through a little gate beside the village hall. Follow the path across a small paddock, going fairly close to the

106

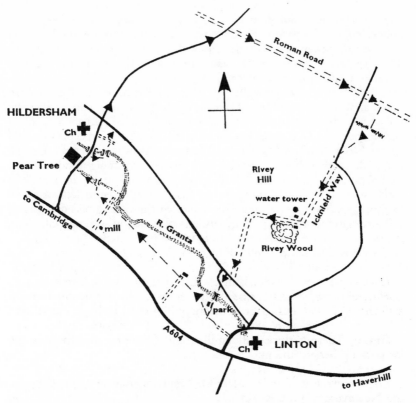

river. Turn left over a substantial wooden bridge, cross a boggy piece of land and bear left at the waymark. Go over a stile into a lane. When you reach the tarmac turn left for 10 yards then right, up a bank and along a broad headland path, with a hedge on the left, to reach a road at right angles. Turn left and walk to the crossroads, then turn right towards Balsham.

Go along the road for about 1 mile, climbing steadily after the first ½ mile. Very soon after going under grid lines, go right off the road, along a cart track by a 'Circular Walk' waymark. About 20 yards after leaving the road the cart track becomes a green lane. This is Roman Road.

About a mile along the ancient track, cross straight over a road and continue, still on Roman Road. At first the track has a hedge on the right and a ditch on the left. Halfway to the next cross-hedge, which you can see on the left, go right through a wide gap in the hedge on the right and follow the path, across the field, to a gap in the next hedge. The route of the walk now follows the Icknield Way (Walkers Route).

At the next cross-hedge change direction, slightly to rightish, now heading towards a clump of trees in a little dip, and to the right of an old water tower on top of the hill. At the far side of the field bear left on the road, and where it turns sharp left, close to the entrance to Chilford Hall Vineyard, go straight ahead on a gravel road up the hill. At the top, pass the water tower on the right.

On reaching a wood in front, where the ground starts to slope down towards Linton, turn right along a broad cart track. Nearby is a flint-faced cottage, a reminder that we are on chalk, where flint used to be a major building material. Continue beside the wood and, where the wood on the left ends, keep straight on along the ridge for about 150 yards. At the waymark the cart track turns left, down the hill towards Linton.

When you reach the road turn right and pass the telephone exchange on the right. Turn down Crabtree Croft. At the end of the cul-de-sac, keep straight on along a tarmac footpath. Pass on the left the flint and brick building called Symonds House. On reaching the road cross straight over, still on a tarmac footpath. Go over the river Granta and keep on the footpath across the recreation ground, passing a pavilion on the right. At the far side of the recreation ground, leave the tarmac and go right, with the boundary of the playing field on the left and a children's play area with its aerial ropeway on the right.

Leave the recreation ground and cross the unusual clapper stile. Go through a new kissing-gate and then on a wide footpath between paddocks. Go out through another kissing-gate to cross over a newish road. On the right is a house and a large farm with some old barns. Then go straight on along a broad cart track, passing, about 100 yards away on the right, more flint cottages.

Keep on the wide, grassy track, with a mature hedge on the left and an open field on the right. Note the mature oak trees in the fields here. Go under the grid lines. Pass a small coppice on the left, then a water treatment plant, also on the left. The track continues broad and grassy, but with a hedge on the right. Soon the path follows the bank of the river Granta on the right, for a few yards. Half-left, on a hill, is an old windmill, with an attractive ogee'd cap.

Cross straight over a cart track, with grass in the middle, which leads to the windmill and keep on the broad, grassy track, with a hedge on the right. In 100 yards go right, through the hedge and over a stile, and then go half-left. When you get to two footbridges across the stream on your right, do not go over either of them but keep parallel to the river, which will lead out to the road. Turn right to return to the Pear Tree.

Other local attractions: Linton Zoo is situated on the Hadstock road, just a few yards south of the A604 in Linton. Opening hours are from 10 am to 6 pm, or dusk, on 364 days a year. Telephone: 01839 222003. No dogs or pets inside the zoo, only in the car park.

108

26 Wicken
The Maid's Head

Wicken is a small fenland settlement not far from the river Cam. The older dwellings of the village are grouped around the green, alongside which is a pretty pond. To the south, lies a tract of uncultivated fen, which was once part of Wicken's common land. It has remained in its almost natural state for many years, having originally been used by the villagers for peat cutting and for reeds for thatching. Part of this fen was bought by the National Trust as early as 1899 and now, together with subsequent acquisitions, is a nature reserve, an area of marsh intersected by drainage ditches where trees, bushes and water-loving plants live side by side. It is a rich habitat for wildlife. In marked contrast, the surrounding area, apart from Wicken Fen, is a broad expanse of fertile agricultural land criss-crossed with wide drainage ditches. Over the years the peat has dried and shrunk and the present arable fields are at a noticeably lower level than the land in the reserve.

The Maid's Head stands back from the main road, in a delightful setting at the corner of a row of cottages, several thatched, which face the green and its border of chestnut trees. It was built in 1760 and has always been the village pub. Around 1983 it suffered a serious fire and the damaged parts were rebuilt. The part-thatched inn has a friendly

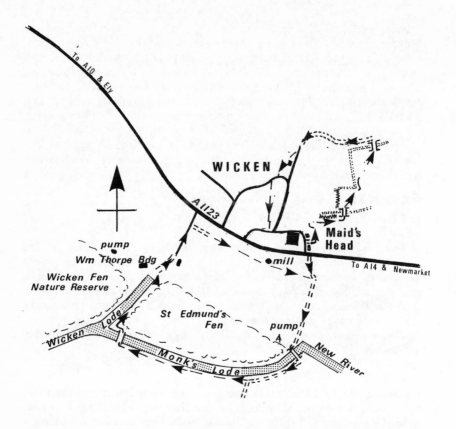

atmosphere. A large free-standing log fire in the middle of the lounge bar glows and warms the whole area on cold days, the smoke going up a conical black hood above it. Small tables dotted around give an informal air. Up three steps at the end of the lounge bar is the more formal restaurant, with sparkling glassware and pink napery, making a fine show. Outside, there is a garden area where children can play.

Both the printed menu and the blackboard of specials are designed to set the gastric juices flowing. For instance, there is half a roast pheasant in a red wine sauce, seafood pancakes topped with cheese, medallions of pork sautéed, and served with a mustard and brandy sauce, and a darne of Scottish salmon placed on a sauce of dill, shallots and cream. Special menus are available for vegetarians and for children. The real ales served are Bass, Worthington Best Bitter and a guest ale. Red Rock draught cider is also on offer. Normal opening times apply here. Dogs are allowed in the public bar.

Telephone: 01353 720727.

How to get there: Wicken lies on the A1123 road between Stretham and Soham. From all directions except the east, follow the A10 Cambridge to King's Lynn road. At Stretham, which is about 5 miles south of Ely, turn south-east at a roundabout, on the A1123 towards Newmarket for about 5 miles. From the east, take the A142 Newmarket to Ely road and turn on to the A1123 at a roundabout about 6 miles north of Newmarket. The Maid's Head is on the main road in the centre of the village.

Parking: The Maid's Head has its own large car park. In addition, the National Trust has a car park close to the entrance to the Wicken Fen nature reserve.

Length of the walk: 3 miles. Map: OS Landranger sheet 154 Cambridge and Newmarket (inn GR 571706).

This 3 mile walk comprises two loops which meet at the Maid's Head. The first loop of 2 miles takes a track to the corner of St Edmund's Fen, where there are two wind pumps (one derelict). The walk follows along the side of the fen on the bank of a wide and placid waterway known as Monk's Lode, and then beside another known as Wicken Lode, to the entrance of the National Trust nature reserve, and returns to the village, passing an old tower mill.

The second loop of the walk crosses the rich arable land to the north of Wicken, with distant views of the village of Soham.

The Walk

From the Maid's Head, cross the green and turn left along the main road for a few yards. Turn right at the footpath sign along a tarmac road, Grass Green. When the tarmac ends keep straight on along a grassy cart track until you reach a wide watercourse and a nearby wind pump on a steel gantry beside a similar, derelict, structure. Ignore the small bridge and stile leading to the left but in about 10 yards cross the wide channel and turn right to follow the bank, with the waterway on the right. This river is known as Monk's Lode. It is a drainage channel which has its source near to Newmarket and flows into the river Cam about a mile away.

Where the track turns left and goes straight to Priory Farm, ¼ mile away, cross a stile and continue alongside Monk's Lode. Cross another stile and in 100 yards turn right and cross the waterway by a wooden cartbridge. This bridge marks the end of the navigable waterway from the river Cam. Now follow the water on the left, bearing round to the right on the bank of Wicken Lode. In ¼ mile reach the entrance to the Wicken Fen nature reserve.

Continue on the tarmac road, passing the National Trust car park and, about 100 yards from the end of this road, turn right at a footpath sign along Back Lane. At first it is a tarmac track, then it gradually gets narrower until it leads into a grass path. Keep on, to pass the tower mill on the left and, shortly after, go through a kissing-gate into a field. Follow the hedge on the left and turn left at a cart track. You are now on the route along which you started. Go out to the road and the Maid's Head.

Cross the main road and go down Butts Lane, with the green and the Maid's Head on the left. After the first few cottages on the right, go right at the footpath sign on a track for a few yards and then go left on a waymarked headland path. Continue round the field until, after a left turn, you cross a stile and a wooden footbridge into the corner of a large field. From this corner turn half-right and cross to a yellow waymark at an internal corner of the field. Keep the field ditch on your left for about 50 yards and turn 30° to the right, across the field, in the direction indicated by another waymark, to a wooden bridge and a stile.

Here turn left on a narrow, grassy footpath between hedges, back towards the village. You join a concrete road, close to a small pumping station, and in a few yards swing right, onto a grass path, keeping to the right of a house. The path leads to a road where you turn right.

In 40 yards turn left at a footpath sign onto a track and into a field. Keep the field boundary on the left and, at the corner of the field, keep straight on between fences. This is a very narrow path which, after making a sharp left and right turn between garden walls, comes out to a road at the corner of the green, quite close to the village pond. Turn left along the road, back to the Maid's Head.

Other local attractions: Wicken Fen is open all the year except Christmas Day. The William Thorpe building which is passed on the walk, at the entrance to Wicken Fen nature reserve, houses a visitor centre describing the history of, and the work that goes on in, Wicken Fen. Nearby is Fen Cottage (NT), open on Sundays from April to October, 2 pm to 5 pm.

27 Littleport
The Black Horse

Littleport is a small town standing on a slight hill about 60 ft above the surrounding fens, 5 miles north of the cathedral city of Ely. The main street drops gently down to the Great Ouse, which flows northwards to the Wash by King's Lynn. The river is an important waterway and is well used by narrow boats and other pleasure craft in the summer. Cargo barges occasionally ply up and down.

The Black Horse is on the river front beside a bridge over the Great Ouse. It is very quiet here in winter, but in summer there are many boats to watch. There is a children's play area by the water (young children would obviously need careful supervision).

If you like hot, spicy food you will enjoy the food here, though of course there are more temperate dishes on the menu. Examples of what is on offer are sirloin steak with hot Mexican sauce, or with a creamed mushroom and brandy sauce, spicy beef (Ternera Picante), chicken wings in brandy, half a pheasant with grapes, spicy chicken, chicken in garlic (Pollo al Ajillo), red snapper, swordfish and a choice of sweets. On Sundays a traditional Sunday lunch is served. The pub offers a changing selection of real ales, always a choice of three. Scrumpy Jack

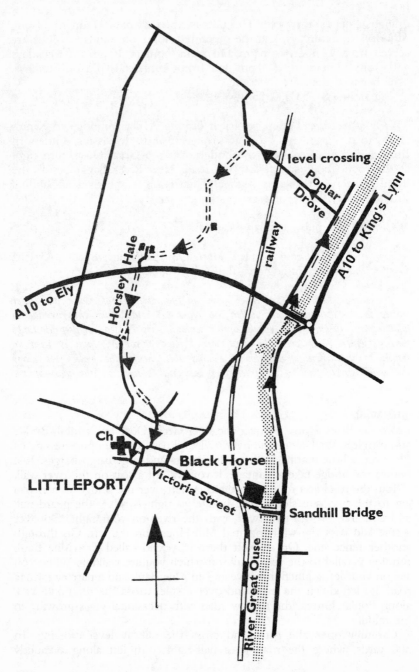

level crossing

Poplar Drove

railway

A10 to King's Lynn

A10 to Ely

Horsley Hale

Ch

Black Horse

LITTLEPORT

Victoria Street

Sandhill Bridge

River Great Ouse

draught cider is also sold. The pub is open all day, 11 am to 11 pm, Mondays to Saturdays, and the permitted hours on Sundays. Meals are served from 12 noon to 3 pm and from 7 pm to 10 pm on weekdays and from 12 noon to 2.30 pm and from 7 pm to 10 pm on Sundays. Well behaved dogs are welcome.

Telephone: 01353 860328.

How to get there: Littleport is just off the A10 Cambridge to King's Lynn road. From Ely, follow the main A10, bypassing Littleport. Immediately after crossing the bridge over the Great Ouse, turn right at the roundabout and follow the road, New River Bank, beside the flood protection bank for ¾ mile. Then re-cross the river at Sandhill Bridge to the Black Horse.

Parking: The pub has a large car park.

Length of the walk: 4½ miles. Map: OS Landranger sheet 143 Ely, Wisbech and surrounding area (inn GR 576864).

The walk starts on the east bank of the river Great Ouse and later crosses to the opposite bank. After 1½ miles the route leaves the riverside to follow paths through rich, black arable fenland, criss-crossed by deep drainage ditches. After going over the Littleport bypass a country lane is used to return to the centre of the town. Beyond the church, the walk goes along the main street, passing an interesting memorial plaque on the wall of the library.

The Walk

From the Black Horse go over the river Great Ouse by Sandhill Bridge and turn left. Walk along the river wall, and pass, on the opposite side of the river, a little marina, with small cruisers and large cargo barges. Just before the bridge take advantage, if you will, of a seat on the river wall.

Join the road at a roundabout and go left over the bridge. When you get to the opposite side of the bridge go right, striding the guard rail, and continue on the river wall, with the river on your right. Go over a stile and pass the white-painted Mill House on the left. Go through another fence line. On the left there is a road called Ten Mile Bank running parallel to the river bank on which you are walking. When you see on your left a junction between Ten Mile Bank and a narrow tarmac road, go left down the bank and over a stile. Cross the road and walk along Poplar Drove, the narrow road with occasional grass growing in the middle.

Carefully open the gates and cross the railway level crossing. In 300 yards, where the road goes half-right, turn left along a muddy

115

cart track, with a deep drainage channel on the left. The ditch on the left ends and from there the track bears round to the left. After passing a farm on the left, the track becomes a narrow tarmac road. Come to a farm building on the right and then bear left for a few yards along Horsley Hale out to a road, the A10, close by a complicated looking roadside weather station. Cross straight over the main road and continue along the track, towards the town.

When you reach a radio mast, or the remains of one, and buildings in front of you, immediately bear left and leave the narrow tarmac road on a grassy headland track, with a cupressus hedge on the right. The track lies at the top of a bank which falls away on the right. Join a gravel road, with a bungalow on the left. Then cross a concrete road, and continue ahead on a grass path, with a ranch-style fence on the left and a house on the right. Go through a little paddock and keep straight on, with buildings on both sides.

The path leads into a residential road, with a long terrace of houses on the left. Pass the end of Mow Fen Road on the left and in 100 yards bear right at the Y-junction. Soon pass Littleport Fire Station. Reach another Y-junction, close to the 'LITTLEPORT' town sign which displays the church, river, windmill and a sailing boat. Go right and immediately right again on the road towards Welney. Very shortly, go left opposite the old school, passing St George's church on the right, and turn left.

At the crossroads go straight on into Main Street. The Crown is on the left. Pass Granby Street on the left and you are now in Victoria Street by the library, an old building, on the wall of which is a memorial to James William Maghtall, son of Littleport and a railwayman. He was posthumously awarded the George Cross for his heroism in saving the people and town of Soham from death and destruction on 2nd June 1944. He was 22. His driver was badly injured. They removed a blazing wagon laden with bombs from an ammunition train. The memorial was erected by Network South East in 1992, to record the Guns Act and to mark the electrification of the Cambridge to King's Lynn railway line.

Keep straight on along Victoria Street for ½ mile. Go over the railway crossing to return to the Black Horse and your start.

28 Burwell
The Five Bells

The villages of Burwell, Reach and Swaffham Prior lie about 10 miles to the east of Cambridge on the edge of the Cambridgeshire Fens, in the eastern part of the county. The land to the south of these settlements rises gradually to the chalk grasslands of Newmarket Heath.

Burwell is a large village, just a few miles from Newmarket. The large St Mary's church stands at one end of the village close to the ruins of Burwell Castle. Reach was once a port with vessels plying up and down Reach Lode. It had access across the wetlands to the sea at the Wash.

The Five Bells is a welcoming pub, with two bars and a restaurant. It was a mid 18th century coaching inn and the stables still exist at the rear of the yard. There is a family room, and a play area outside for children.

Much of the food is home-made. One may choose from quiche lorraine, chicken curry, gammon steak and eggs, crispy mushrooms, goujons of plaice or mixed grill, with strawberry cheesecake, sticky orange fudge cake, exotic fruit gâteau or raspberry pavlova to follow. The parsnip and apple soup served here is delectable. Traditional Sunday lunch is a feature. Real ales on call at this Greene King pub are Greene King IPA, Abbot and Mild. Dry Blackthorn draught cider is also available. The pub is open normal hours, and all day

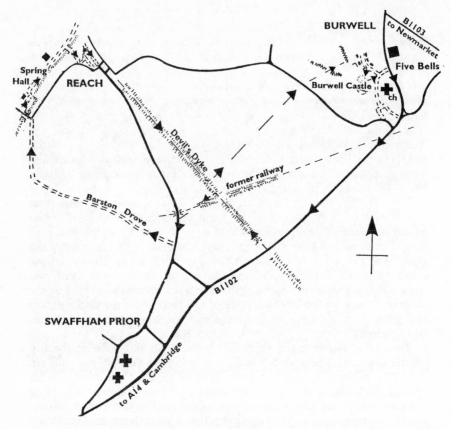

on Saturday. Lunches and evening meals are served every day except Monday. Well-behaved dogs may go inside.

Telephone: 01638 741404.

How to get there: Leave the A14 Cambridge to Bury road at the grade-separated interchange on the east side of Cambridge, signed 'Burwell' and 'Cambridge' and, approaching from the west, also 'Newmarket'. Take the B1102 road through Swaffham Prior and in a further 2 miles reach Burwell. The Five Bells is on the right just beyond the church.

Parking: Cars can be parked in the yard behind the pub, in front of it, or in the village street.

Length of the walk: 5½ miles. Map: OS Landranger sheet 154 Cambridge and Newmarket (inn GR 589662).

The walk is to the village of Reach. It follows the Devil's Dyke for a short distance through the nature reserve and then leaves the Dyke to go to the edge of Swaffham Prior. Here a 1½ mile detour can be made into the village. The walk continues along a droveway on the edge of the fen to Reach. The return is along the Devil's Dyke and across fields to Burwell, passing the ditches and banks which are all that is left of the 12th century Burwell Castle built over an earlier Roman settlement.

The Walk

Leave the Five Bells and walk along the main road, passing the church on the right. In a short distance pass Isaacson Road on the left and keep straight on towards Swaffham Prior. About 1 mile from the pub, the road intersects the rampart of the Devil's Dyke.

The Devil's Dyke is an ancient, possibly Roman, defensive earthwork which runs for 7 miles across this band of open chalklands. It is one of several parallel fortifications which were thrown up to protect East Anglia from raiders from the west. The Dyke ends at Reach because the fenland to the north would have been impassable to an enemy. At the other end, at Woodditton, the land beyond the Dyke to the south was impenetrable woods and forest. Pause for a few moments to look at the ditch and bank on the left-hand side of the road. Here the undergrowth and other vegetation has been cleared and you can appreciate the scale of the earthworks.

Turn right and in a few yards climb the bank and walk on the top of the rampart. The area is a nature reserve. As you go you will see distantly, on the left, the two windmills of Swaffham Prior. In just under ½ mile, the Dyke is crossed by the route of a former railway line. Here the path swings left down some steps to the level of the former railway. Cross the cutting and climb again through a blackthorn thicket. When you are almost back at the top of the rampart, at a waymark, turn left and go down steps which lead into a field at the foot of the Dyke. Follow the headland path, with the former railway on the left. The path soon swings left, obliquely crossing the old railway cutting and climbing out the other side into a pleasant tree belt. The path leads out to a road.

Turn left along the road. In 50 yards, at a signpost, turn right along a broad cart track. Should you wish to explore Swaffham Prior, an interesting village, with attractive buildings on both sides of the main street and two churches within the same churchyard, keep straight on the road (¾ mile) and return to this point to continue the walk.

Follow the cart track, signed 'Devil's Dyke Walks', at first with a thick hedge on the left and later a hedge on the right. The track, known as Barston Drove, becomes a wide grassy path, which, after swinging round to the right, reaches a narrow tarmac road at a sharp bend. Turn left on the road for a few yards to cross the bridge over a drainage ditch, and, almost immediately, turn right at the byway sign along the track to

Spring Hall. Pass the farm and continue on a grass track beside the ditch on the right. Soon pass Rose Cottage on the left, with its large pargeted plaster rose on the front wall. When you come to a concrete slab bridge over the ditch, turn right, cross the ditch and enter the village of Reach.

At the road, swing left and in 20 yards turn half-left along a narrow tarmac footpath. Keep left where the path divides and go out to a road. Turn right and walk up to the village green. Go past the village sign. The King's Dyke End public house is on the opposite side of the green. Pass the chestnut tree. At the far end of the green you reach the end of the Devil's Dyke. Pass the footpath sign and in 50 yards climb the Dyke.

Keep on the narrow footpath on the top of the bank for just over ½ mile. Take the steps which lead down the bank on the left, close by an electricity pole, and follow a track straight towards Burwell, to reach a road in ½ mile. Cross straight over and take the field path to Burwell. You bear slightly right from the previous direction to cross the field towards two separate wooden electricity poles in the opposite hedge. Go through the hedge beside the poles and continue in the same direction, on a headland path with a ditch on the left. Half-right you can see the low ramparts of the castle and behind them, the church.

At the far side of the field go left over a concrete slab bridge and continue in the same direction as before, this time with a hedge on the right. In the corner, at the footpath sign, turn right along a narrow footpath between hedges. The path, after several bends, leads to a narrow road with houses opposite. Turn right and, in about 10 yards, enter the field on the right through a kissing-gate. This field contains the remains of Burwell Castle. Keep left, skirting the castle remains on the right. Just beyond the exit kissing-gate, in the shadow of the boundary wall, a stream bubbles up out of the ground, and through a pipe now, to feed Burwell Lode which later discharges into the river Cam. This spring is the 'well' from which Burwell gets its name. Leave the field by a gate opposite a school-like building, very close to the church.

In the churchyard, due west of the church and south of the schoolroom, among the older graves, is a particularly poignant one. On the back of the headstone is a heart borne up by wings and surmounted by flames, with a skull and bones carved beneath. On the other side is engraved, 'To the memory of the 78 people who were burnt to death in a barn at Burwell on Sept 5th 1727'. They had been watching a magic show, and the magician's table was pushed against the barn doors, blocking the exit, when a match set the hay in the barn alight. In 1727 those 78 people must have been quite a large proportion of the population.

From the castle area kissing-gate bear left, follow the churchyard wall, and at the road by the village pump, turn left, back to the Five Bells and your start.

Castle Camps
The Cock

In the extreme south-east corner of Cambridgeshire, bordering both Essex and Suffolk, lies the village of Castle Camps. It is a small, pretty place, barely 5 miles from the Suffolk town of Haverhill. The surrounding area is gently undulating farmland, intersected by shallow valleys.

The friendly, pinky-white, slate-roofed Cock is a compact building, even though it has been extended forwards, as you can appreciate by the unusual ceiling levels inside. As you look up to the ceiling you can see the large display of blue plates.

The home-cooked food includes jumbo cod and chips, steak pie, chicken hoisin, which includes bean sprouts, cress and cashew nuts, beef curry and rice, chilli con carne, scampi and chips, chicken pot pie and various omelettes. To follow, there is apple strudel and cream, treacle or chocolate pudding. The real ales served are Greene King IPA and Abbot and Nethergate. Dry Blackthorn cider is available, too. The pub is open during the usual hours and all day on Saturdays. Food is served at lunchtime and in the evenings up to 9.30 pm, seven days a week. Reservations are taken for Sunday lunch. There is a garden.

Telephone: 01799 584207.

How to get there: Make your way to the roundabout junction between the A11 Newmarket to London road and the A604 Cambridge to Colchester road. Then follow the A604 for 4 miles and take the turning, right, to Bartlow. Keep straight on to Castle Camps and at the village sign turn left. The Cock is about 300 yards away on the left.

Parking: The pub has its own car park at the rear.

Length of the walk: 4½ miles. Map: OS Landranger sheet 154 Cambridge and Newmarket (inn GR 633434).

The walk starts by going to the church, All Saints church, of flint construction, which stands on a rise below where the castle was. The tower is in a parlous state, so mind your head as you walk round. There are some delicately carved heads, mask-stops, at the terminals of some of the window dripstones, which have withstood the onslaught of the elements. Beside the church, Castle Farm stands on a mound surrounded by a deep ditch. This is the site of an ancient motte and bailey, the former castle, which, no doubt, figures in the village name. Passing Castle Farm, the walk continues across farmland to the county boundary, on a slight hill with wide views to the south, and returns through a hamlet called Camps End, over the tiny river Granta, here not far from its source, and along a grassy track back to the Cock.

The Walk
From the Cock go right, straight down the High Street. Pass the nonconformist church, with a clock on its gable end, on the left. At the T-junction by the village sign and a war memorial, turn left for about 20 yards and, at a footpath sign, turn right along a gravel cart track. Pass a pair of brick cottages on the right and follow a pleasant grass path towards a radio mast on the skyline. On the far side of the field go over a narrow culvert to join another path and immediately turn right, with a little ditch on the right and a fence on the left. The path is soon a grass headland with a ditch on the left. After passing some bushes, the lovely grass path lies along a bank, making directly for the church. Go over a culvert with a handrail, past a public seat. At the approach to the church go through a steel kissing-gate into a pasture and carry on in the same direction as before, leaving the field by a wooden kissing-gate and out to a lane beside the church.

Turn left along the farm drive to Castle Farm, up the hill, or cut through the churchyard and go out at the top by a little gate in the south wall. Castle Farm lies ahead on a moat-surrounded mound. Turn right and cross the stile beside the churchyard wall into a pasture.

There are two parallel ditches in this field, probably once part of the defences. Go half-left round the end of the first ditch and then

122

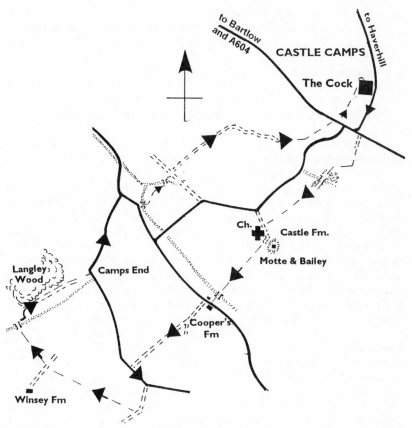

to Bartlow and A604

to Haverhill

CASTLE CAMPS

The Cock

Langley Wood

Camps End

Ch.

Castle Fm.

Motte & Bailey

Cooper's Fm

Winsey Fm

half-right to a narrow path between some bushes through a gap at the second ditch. At the far side of the grass field, cross a stile into an arable field. Go straight across this field, at right angles to the hedge you have just crossed. When you get over the rise in the ground you can see your destination. You are making for the middle of a machinery storage area in front of the barns of Cooper's Farm.

Cross a sleeper bridge over a ditch and then go through the implement yard and out to the road in front of the large barns. Turn right along the road for 20 yards and then turn left, at a footpath sign, up a concrete farm track beside newish barns on the left, and a pink house on the right. Follow a cart track, it gets more and more grassy, with a ditch on the left. At the point where the main cart track goes left across a culvert over a ditch towards a small copse of fir trees, leave the main track and keep straight on, still with a ditch on the left. The path turns into a tarmac lane. Pass on the left Hazelberry Cottage, beautifully pargeted and pink, and thatched Spindleberry Cottage. Meet a road and turn left. In 200 yards or so, where the road makes a bend to the left towards Charlwood Farm, go right on a grassy lane between hedges. The lane comes out into the corner of a big field stretching away in front and to the left. Here is the Essex county boundary.

Leave the lane, turn right, cross a culvert and follow the ditch on the right. Where the ditch turns right, away from the path, go straight on, curving slightly to the right towards a pollarded ash. Go over a culvert in the shade of the ash and then continue on a headland path, with a ditch on the right. Where the hedge on the right turns right, keep straight on across the field. Cross the farm road leading to Winsey Farm and continue on the headland, with a hedge on the right.

The path drops down into a shallow valley. At the bottom of the valley, cross a stream and then turn right, with the stream on the right. At the next field boundary go left on a headland, with the hedge on the right, up to Langley Wood. At the corner of the wood turn right on a pleasant grassy cart track and follow the edge of the trees on the left. When you reach the corner of the wood on the left, keep straight on along the cart track. Go over a stile and then follow a fence on the right, out to the road by a letter box.

Go left along the road, bearing round to the right and down the hill. Pass a prominent blue-painted, thatched cottage. When you come to a T-junction, turn right on the road signposted 'Olmstead Green and the Bumpsteads'. Where the road turns sharp right, you leave it, keeping straight on at a footpath sign and over a bridge over a stream. Climb 20 yards or so and turn left through a hedge, then continue on a headland path, following the stream on the left. Continue round the field, still following the stream, and when you come to the diagonally opposite corner of this field go left over a concrete bridge across the young river Granta and up some steps. Continue for 50 yards, with the river on the right.

At the cart track, where there is, on the right, a bridge over the stream, turn left away from the river for 10 yards, then go right on a path beside a hedge on the left. Follow the wide, grass path, along the headland of a long field. At the far end of the field the grass path goes over a culvert and continues alongside a ditch on the left. Follow the ditch round to the right and in about 100 yards you go left over a narrow culvert on a reinstated path towards a row of cupressus trees opposite, across a field. Keep beside the cupressus and then follow a fence on the left, out to the road.

Turn right. In 50 yards turn left onto a narrow cinder path between hedges. Make your way across this next field to the diagonally opposite corner, by an electricity pole with a transformer hanging from it. Go out through a kissing-gate to the green beside the Cock Inn.

124

30 Woodditton
The Three Blackbirds

Woodditton is a small village on the eastern edge of Cambridgeshire, just a few miles south of Newmarket. Many of the houses and their garden walls are made of flints, as in Norfolk. The country around is gently undulating, and much of the land is devoted to stud farms, raising bloodstock for nearby Newmarket. Woodditton lies at the southern end of the Devil's Dyke, the 7 mile long chalk embankment built to defend the inhabitants of East Anglia from the tribes to the west. It did not extend further because the thickly wooded land to the south presented a major natural barrier to an enemy. Even today the countryside around here seems to be well endowed with woods and isolated trees.

The thatched pub has the date 1642 emblazoned on the front wall. On each gable end two pentice boards are to be seen. They are to divert rain water away from the wall – not to cater for perching pigeons! The building has been restored after it was 'modernised' earlier in the century. The lovely old beams have been revealed again and, because of that, the unusual ceiling pargeting between the beams inside the house can now be seen. Was that the forerunner of artex ceilings, but more beautiful? There is, we are told, a resident ghost, a most benign one,

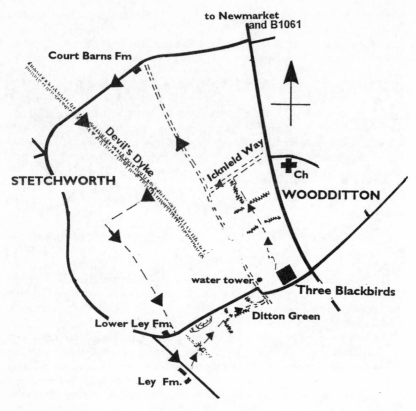

whose footsteps are sometimes heard. The pub has a very cheerful, welcoming atmosphere. People come from far and wide to enjoy the good food and company – witness the vast collection of business cards on the walls, and hundreds in boxes on shelves. Earthenware flagons hang from the beams, together with an unusual collection of traps, and of old flat irons. The bar area is in the front of the pub, with a large restaurant behind, in what was the old brewhouse in days when the pub brewed its own beer. Further seating is upstairs. Outside, in front of the knapped-flint barn, is a pleasant area with tables for warm sunny days, and a garden area for children. As befits a pub in an area dominated by horseracing, the tablemats are pictures of famous racehorses.

The home-made food makes one wish to return again. On the wide-ranging menu are escalopes of pork topped with asparagus, cheese and ham, lamb oriental, chicken breast in a white wine and grain mustard sauce, pieces of Scotch beef casseroled in Guinness and topped with puff pastry, and vegetarian dishes aplenty. Sweets, such as apple pie, banana split, peach melba, mud pie, profiteroles, Death-by-Chocolate and much more, are there to tempt you. The real ales served are Greene King and the draught cider is Dry Blackthorn. The pub is open at lunchtime and in the evenings seven days a week. Dogs are not welcome in the pub.

Telephone: 01638 730811.

How to get there: Woodditton is 3 miles south of Newmarket. At Newmarket go on the A1304 (the main shopping street) to the western end of the town. Here turn off onto the B1061, but in 300 yards, where the B1061 turns right, keep straight on to reach Woodditton. Turn right to the Three Blackbirds.

Parking: Parking at the front of the pub is limited, but the rear car park is large.

Length of the walk: 4½ miles. Map: OS Landranger sheet 154 Cambridge and Newmarket (inn GR 659581).

The route circles to the north through farmland to reach the Icknield Way, the long distance path which goes south-east towards Ivinghoe Beacon to join the Ridgeway path across southern England. After following the Icknield Way for ¼ mile, the walk continues northwards to the Devil's Dyke.

The route returns southwards along the crest of the Dyke. The ancient inhabitants of East Anglia, who originally dug the ditch, formed an embankment with the excavated chalk alongside it. Now it is an attractive strip of land, covered with many trees and shrubs, an important habitat for the flora of the chalk downland and a pleasing area for walking. After going along the top of the embankment for ½ mile, the walk goes nearly into Stetchworth and then returns to the south of Woodditton village centre.

The Walk

Leave the car park at the rear of the pub, walking away from it through a meadow, and at the end go left over a two-sleeper footbridge and immediately turn right. Follow the hedge on your right and make for the far right corner of this big field. Cross a culvert in the corner into another field, with fine views ahead. Heading slightly right of straight ahead, cross the field, going directly towards a tall oak, beside a clump of smaller trees, on the far side. A broad gap takes you in 30 yards to the corner of a big field. Follow the headland path beside the hedge on your left to the end of the field, where you meet the Icknield Way, a cart track, at right angles.

Turn left to follow the Icknield Way, on the track, with a hedge on the left, down the hill and at the bottom meet another farm track at a T-junction, beside the end of a shelter belt.

Go right along the track. After some 200 yards ignore the steps down on your left where the Icknield Way continues. The rising land on your right is copiously planted with young trees. Carry on to the track's end, exiting beside wide green metal gates alongside the vast grey and green Court Barns Farm. On the road go left and climb the hill towards a belt of woodland. Just before the crest of the hill, leave the road at a footpath sign, going left up a bank onto the Devil's Dyke. Follow this ridge for just over a mile through light woodland.

Shortly after going down some steps, crossing a wooden bridge and climbing up the other side, you come to a cross-track. Here turn right, on the Icknield Way once more. With a large field on the left, walk alongside the woodland on the right until it ends. You are now within sight of Stetchworth ahead. Turn left at the wood's corner, by the footpath signpost, and walk with a hedge and ditch on your right. Later pass through a cross-hedge and, later still, a staggered cross-ditch and continue, with a fast-flowing stream on the right. Go out to the road beside wide, green metal farm gates, and turn right.

Pass Lower Ley Farm and then turn left on the tarmac road, signed 'Stetchworth Ley' (ley means grassland). Pass on the right a brick barn and, just by the farm entrance, a sign reads 'Ley Farm'. Turn left over a culvert and walk straight across the field. Aim a bit to the left of the water tower away in Woodditton. Go across the field towards the far boundary. You may see a small red stick over there. This marks a two-sleeper footbridge over a deep ditch, which you cross. Continue across the next field, heading now a little to the right of the water tower, towards the corner of the field.

Just before the corner, pick up a hedge on the right and, in the corner, go straight on through the hedge and through a post and rail fence. Walk on through the paddock, with a hedge and fence on the right. Leave the paddock by a gate which leads into a hardcore track. Walk out to flint-faced cottages and go left for 20 yards to the road. Turn right and walk back to the Three Blackbirds.